LIO AGE

D1469767

The Labradoodle
Handbook

LINDA WHITWAM

ISBN-13: 978-1484008409

Acknowledgements

My sincere thanks to all the Labradoodle owners, organisations and canine experts without whom this book would not have been possible. Special thanks to The Labradoodle Trust UK, Jo Cousins and International Doodle Owners Group (IDOG) and Doodle Rescue Collective Inc (DRC).

This book is dedicated to Jean and Ken

Copyright

Author's Note: For ease of reading, the Labrador Retriever is referred to as the Labrador throughout this book, and the masculine pronoun he is intended to represent both male and female dogs.

Contents

1: The Labradoodle

So, you've been bitten by the Doodle bug? You're one of many thousands of dog lovers who have been captivated by this stunning crossbreed which has enjoyed a meteoric rise to fame.

Since Australian Wally Conron first crossed a Standard Poodle with a Labrador in 1988 and coined the phrase 'Labradoodle', this honest, sociable and fun-loving canine has made his home at the centre of families across the globe.

Originating in Australia, the Labradoodle has become extremely popular elsewhere, particularly in the USA, Canada and the UK. The Labradoodle is a crossbreed, so there are no official statistics as to the number of them in individual countries, as these are based on the registration of pure breeds provided by the Kennel Clubs.

However, you won't go far without spotting some signs of a Labradoodle, everybody knows somebody who's got one, or they see them around their neighbourhood.

The media hype on TV and in the Press has been enormous. Unfortunately this - and the fact that Labradoodles have been promoted by some as being perfectly suitable for all allergy sufferers - has led to criticism of this wonderful crossbreed, as well as some unscrupulous breeding to cash in on the craze – but none of this is the fault of the dog.

To set the record straight, as the Kennel Clubs will tell anyone who asks, there is no such thing as a totally non-shedding dog. There are however, certain breeds – and in the case of the Labradoodle, a crossbreed - which may be more suitable for allergy sufferers.

Some Labradoodles may be suitable for allergy sufferers, but by no means all. If you suffer from allergies you need to spend time with the individual dog – see **Chapter 4.** Some Labradoodles shed, some shed a little and others, particularly many of the multigeneration Doodles, are 'minimal shedders.'

Well, that's got that out of the way! Let's look at some of the reasons why the Labradooodle is so loved in countries all over the world.

Appearance

Labradoodles come in all shapes, sizes and colours and sport many different coats. But one thing is generally agreed – an ugly Labradoodle has yet to be born.

In extremely general terms, an F1 (first generation) Labradoodle has a scruffy look and multigenerations and Australian Labradoodle look more like teddy bears.

Regardless of what type of Labradoodle you have or are thinking of getting, there is no denying that they are extremely appealing canines. This coupled with their sociable, often amusing personality, loyalty and suitability for family life has all contributed to the Labradoodle's popularity.

Puppies are particularly attractive, so make sure you do your research. Decide exactly what type and size you want first and then pick a good breeder before you decide to view any puppies, as the sight of a litter of fluffy Labradoodle pups may well be too much to resist.

Labradoodles come in three different sizes with three different coat types -and variations within these types. Then you have to decide if you want a Labradoodle or an Australian Labradoodle. When you've finally figured all this out, you then have to decide what F number of dog you want - or whether to go for a multigen.

Sound like a foreign language? Fear not, we will take you by the hand and gently guide you with straightforward words and pictures through the jargon and pitfalls to help you to pick and then care for a Labradoodle who will, with any luck, become a wonderful companion and major part of your life for the next decade or more.

F Numbers

What's all this talk about F numbers? Well, it has nothing at all to do with Formula 1 racing or photography and everything to do with Labradoodles. Here, in a nutshell is F numbers demystified.

The Labradoodle is a crossbreed, not a purebred (North America) or pedigree (UK). It is the product of crossing two breeds of dog: the

Labrador and the Poodle - and a couple of other breeds in the case of the Australian Labradoodle, more on that later.

Because the Labradoodle is a crossbreed, you cannot get papers with your dog which are recognised by the Kennel Clubs. But despite this, you should always find out about your dog's parents and ancestry – because provided you care for him well, his genes will be the major factor in deciding how healthy he will be.

F stands for filial when describing Labradoodles. It comes from the Latin *filius* (son) and means "relating to a son or daughter."

An **F1** Labradoodle is a first generation cross, so one parent was a Labrador and the other was a Poodle. An F1 Labradoodle is more likely to moult than higher generation Labradoodles, as half of its genes are coming from the Labrador, which sheds hair. According to an unofficial Doodle database involving 237 dogs, over half of F1 Labradoodles monitored shed hair to some degree – although many were light shedders and some caused no problems with allergy sufferers.

Some canine experts believe that a first generation cross may benefit from 'hybrid vigour.' This is the belief that the first cross between two unrelated purebred lines is healthier and grows better than either parent line.

The next generations are worked out by always adding one number up from the lowest number parent. Some people believe that hybrid vigour is lost with each successive generation.

An **F2** could be the offspring of two F1 – or first generation - Labradoodles or the product of an F1 x F2, F3 or F4 cross. An **F3** is the offspring of one F2 parent where the other was F2 or higher, for example: F2 xF3 x F2 x F4 Labradoodle. F1B, F2B, F3B etc: The B stands for Backcross.

This occurs when a litter has been produced as a result of a backcross to one of the parent breeds – normally a Poodle (so when a Labradoodle is bred with a Poodle). This is usually done to improve coat type and increase the possibility of a low shedding coat. It is not common practice for breeders to backcross to a Labrador, so a typical F1B might be one quarter Labrador and three quarters Poodle.

A second generation backcross pup (F2B) is the result of a Labradoodle (F1) bred to a Labradoodle backcross (F1B). Although three generations in the making, F2Bs are technically second generation dogs. Here are some examples:

1st generation pup, F1 = Labrador x Poodle
1st generation pup with a backcross, F1B = - Labrador x Poodle
2nd generation pup with a backcross, F2B = Labradoodle backcross x Labradoodle.

All clear?? Well, we're moving on anyway! A **multigen** (or **multigeneration**) Labradoodle is the result of successive Labradoodle to Labradoodle breeding (rather than purebred Labradors and Poodles). However, in practice, backcrosses and Poodles are also used in the early generations. This is why in some older lines of multigeneration Labradoodles have a lot of Poodle in their genetic make-up.

Poodles (like the Toy ones on the previous page) are less expensive and, as they have a wool coat, increase the likelihood of the puppies having a low-shed or non-shedding coat. They also introduce some popular new colours such as red and parti (white and another colour). While hybrid vigour may be lost, the advantage of multigens is that good breeders can reproduce a more consistent size, appearance and coat type by breeding multigen to multigen.

All Australian Labradoodles are multigeneration, but not all multigenerations are Australian Labradoodles.

 Because multigens have become very popular and expensive, with prices sometimes rising to four or even five figures, there are many people who advertise multigens and charge a high price for puppies who are either not technically multigeneration or are not the product of careful breeding. See **Chapter 3. Puppies** on how to select a good breeder and what questions to ask.

'Hybrid Vigour'

Labradoodles and other so-called 'designer dogs' are causing a big debate in the canine world at the moment. Some people think it's a great idea to create a dog by crossing two existing breeds, thereby increasing the gene pool and reducing the risk of inherited problems in puppies.

When done responsibly, breeding is **by design**. In other words, it is breeding between a deliberately chosen sire and dam. This proper parentage can give the crossbreed puppy the advantage of hybrid vigour – or robustness.

The theory is that the puppy may be stronger and healthier as he is less likely to inherit the genetic faults of either purebred parent. Many purebred (pedigree) breeds have health problems which have been bred in over the years.

 For example, some Dalmatians are deaf, some Labradors have hip problems and Dachshunds may suffer from back problems. This is because as well as breeding the good points into a purebred, the faults have also been inadvertently passed on.

However, although the gene pool is larger with crossbreeds like the Labradoodle, health checks still have to be made on the parents, which is why it is so important to get your puppy from an expert Labradoodle breeder. For example, if your Labradoodle pup has a Labrador with hip problems as a parent or ancestor, there is a chance that your puppy will inherit that fault, just as with a purebred.

Size, colour and coat are just some of the variable factors with Labradoodles – even within the same litter. Although Australian Labradoodle breeders, particularly in Australia and the USA, are breeding multigeneration Labradoodles and working towards a consistent breed standard.

Many Labradoodles are sold as non-shedding and hypoallergenic, but no breeder can categorically say their dogs will not shed and you will not be allergic to them. They are, however, more likely to be non-shedding than some other crossbreeds where both parents moult. There are no cast iron guarantees; odds are that even the other littermates didn't turn out exactly the same as your dog.

The idea of **hybrid vigour** is that a first generation (F1) crossbred dog will be healthier than a purebred. Of course, this only applies if both parents are from healthy stock and do not carry any inherent defects.

How wonderful it would be if you could take any two purebred dogs, cross breed them and automatically ensure a 100% healthy dog. Unfortunately, it is not as simple as that.

Some say hybrid vigour is a result of carefully planned breeding based on studying the health and personality histories of the parent dogs over several generations. They also believe that it occurs only in first generation, or F1, crosses.

Others maintain that hybrid vigour does not exist in crossbred dogs. They think that the dog might inherit the health problems of either or both parents. It's fair to say the jury's still out - you'll have to make up your own mind. If you do decide to get a Labradoodle, the most important thing you can do is to select a good, responsible breeder.

Australian Labradoodles Explained

So what's the difference between an Australian Labradoodle and a Labradoodle?

A Labradoodle is a cross between a Labrador and any of the three sizes of Poodle. All of its heritage can be traced back to these two breeds. A Labradoodle can be F1, F2, F3, multigeneration, etc but it will only have Labrador and Poodle genes. An Australian Labradoodle is slightly different.

An Australian Labradoodle also has DNA from other dogs. The early Labrador-Poodle crosses in Australia produced large dogs, but they were often stubborn and wilful with high energy levels.

It was therefore decided to introduce another breed, at first two Irish Water Spaniels were used. Later English and American Cocker Spaniels were introduced.

This not only fitted in with what breeders were trying to achieve in terms of a good temperament, but also added a larger bone structure than the Poodle and, very importantly, the Cocker Spaniel's soft fleece coat. Even today, some breeders are still using Cocker Spaniel in their bloodlines.

The name Australian Labradoodle was first coined in 2004 to describe the lines of multigeneration Labradoodles with long pedigrees, many originating from the two kennels in Australia which started breeding them in the early 1990's These were Tegan Park and Rutland Manor, set up by mother and daughter Beverley Manners and Angela Wetzel Cunningham.

The Australian Labradoodle is popular throughout Australia and the USA, while the UK probably has a higher percentage of Labradoodles. Proper breeding - rather than indiscriminate breeding to cash in on a craze – creates more consistency within litters and a higher likelihood of a non-shedding dog (although no dog is 100% non-shedding), as the coat is one factor experienced breeders consider when selecting their breed stock.

The breed organisations, like the Australian Labradoodle Association (ALA) and the Australian Labradoodle Association of America (ALAA), are working with breeders and Kennel Clubs towards their goal of full recognition of the Australian Labradoodle as a pure breed. This will undoubtedly be an uphill task and one which, if successful, will take many years.

Breed Standard

This has been laid down by the ALA:

General Appearance - Must appear athletic and graceful with a compact body displaying substance with medium boning. Should not appear cloddy or heavy nor overly fine. A distinctive feature of this breed is their coat, which is non-shedding and easy to manage.

Temperament - Extremely clever, sociable, comical, joyful, energetic when free and soft and quiet when handled. They should approach people in a happy friendly manner, keen and easy to train. They should display an intuition about their family members or handler's current emotional state or needs. This ability to "know" is what has made the Australian Labradoodle an excellent dog for individuals with special needs.

Size
Standard - Height at wither: 21 to 24 inches. (not over 25) 53cm to 63cm

Weight: 23kg to 30kg. (50-65lbs)
The ideal size for the female is 21 to 23 inches and the male is 22 to 24 inches.

Medium - Height at wither: 17 to 20 inches. (not over 21) 43cm to 52cm
Weight: 13kg to 20kg. (30-645lbs)
The ideal size for the female is 17 to 19 inches and the male is 18 to 20 inches.

Miniature - Height at wither: 14 to 16 inches. (not over 17) 35cm to 42cm
Weight: 7kg to 13kg. (15-25lbs)

Body - (to wither) as to length (from sternum to point of buttock) should appear square and compact. Deep chest and well sprung. There should be a good tuck up. Loins should be strong and muscular.

Head - Moderately broad with well-defined eyebrows. Stop should be moderate with eyes set well apart. The head should be of moderate width; developed but without exaggeration. Foreface to appear shorter than skull. The head should be clean-cut and free from fleshy cheeks. The whole head must be in proportion to the size of the dog.

Ears - Large, expressive and slightly rounded.

Mouth - Must be a scissor bite. Upper teeth to just overlap the bottom teeth.

Nose - Should be large, of square appearance and fleshy.

Teeth - Scissor bite. Undershot or overshot bite is a major fault. Crowding teeth in miniatures is a fault.

Forequarters - Shoulders blades and upper arms to be the same length, and shoulders should be well laid back. Elbows are set close to the body. Forelegs to be straight when viewed from the front. Toeing in our out is a fault.

Hindquarters - In profile the croup is nearly flat, slight sloping of the croup is acceptable. Stifles should be moderately turned to propel forward movement, and hindquarters well muscled for power in movement. Hock to heel should be strong and short being perpendicular to the ground. View from the rear should be parallel to each other, must not be cow-hocked.

Feet - The feet are of medium size, round with well-arched toes having elastic and thick pads. The feet should not turn in or out.

Tail - The tail should follow the topline in repose or when in motion. It may be carried gaily, but should not curl completely over the back. Tip of tail should not touch the back nor curl upon itself.

Movement - Trotting gait is effortless, smooth, powerful and coordinated in mature dogs. Should have a good reach in front and drive from behind for forward motion. Sound free movement and a light gait are essential.

Faults
Any sign of aggression or dominance to be heavily penalised.

- Fearful, timid, yappy or highly-strung temperaments
- Harsh hair, or any sign of undercoat. Coats must be fleece or wool
- Short or overly thick neck
- A coat which sheds (note: some coat instability during hormonal changes with fertile bitches)
- Possum type or Teapot handle tails
- A long narrow or block head
- Protruding or sunken eyes
- Watery or tearful eyes
- Over or undershot or pincer mouth
- Long back
- Crowding teeth
- Bad carriage or heavy gait
- Monorchid or inverted vulva
- Cow-hock
- Toeing in or out
- Colour, albinism is a disqualification
- Over or under sized is a major fault

As with Australian Labradoodles, there are three sizes of Labradoodles. You must decide which size best fits in with your household and daily routine. Some Standard Labradoodles are extremely large with high energy levels and will require a great deal more daily exercise than a Miniature or even a Medium.

Temperament

Whether Australian or simply Labradoodle, one reason why these dogs have become so popular is their temperament. The Labradoodle combines the gentleness and steadfastness of the Labrador with the intelligence and alertness of the Poodle. The Poodle is also an instinctual dog, which is why sometimes you may wonder how your Labradoodle knows what you are thinking!

Both dogs are loyal and regarded as easy to train and many Labradoodles have been trained to high levels for use as service or therapy dogs.

Your dog's character will be formed on the basis of his temperament combined with his environment. Like humans, he is born with a set of natural character traits, but how he turns out as an adult will also be affected greatly by you and how you treat him.

By nature Labradoodles are sociable, friendly, affectionate and non-aggressive with other dogs. They are generally alert and many of them, particularly Standard Labradoodles, have high energy levels. They love to be with people and at the heart of family life and are therefore not suitable pets to be left alone all day.

Labradoodles are intelligent and highly trainable, but need plenty of mental and physical stimulation. Standards are big dogs and can be boisterous and mischievous. Miniatures are becoming more popular, but still average around 18" in height.

They want nothing more than to please their people and thrive on interaction. They enjoy a challenge, love games and are easily bored. Most Labradoodles love water -and mud – so if you are particularly house proud, a smaller, less active breed might be a better choice.

Labradoodles love to run, swim and fetch. Their energy levels vary greatly, so it's a good idea to try and see the parents as puppies will

generally take after their parents in this respect. They will bark if someone comes to the door, but are watch dogs rather than guard dogs, as they are likely to welcome any intruder with a wagging tail.

Leaving them alone or unstimulated for long periods can lead to poor or destructive behaviour – which is why some end up in rescue centres. Before taking on a Labradoodle, ask yourself if you genuinely can afford the time that this wonderfully friendly, active and often comical dog deserves.

As with all dogs they need to be treated with respect and need to be given firm, fair training and handling from a very early age, or they will try to outsmart you.

They can sometimes be too intelligent for their own good, but ask any Labradoodle owner and they will say that these dogs are worth their weight in gold.

They often do well with other dogs, and often cats and other animals, due to their natural non-aggressive nature. They also usually do well with children -with a few provisos.

Labradoodles and Children

Because of their non-aggressive and playful temperaments, Labradoodles are highly popular as family pets. Sociable dogs which thrive on being with others, Doodles have carved out a place for themselves at the centre of family life.

There are, however, instances when it doesn't work out and the dog has to be given away. Sometimes this is a result of unforeseen tension between the dog and the kids. If you have children - especially young ones - take time to fully consider the implications before taking on a new canine member of the family.

This is what the UK Doodle Trust (formerly the Labradoodle Trust) has to say about Labradoodles and young children:

"Buying a dog or puppy when you have a very young family needs careful consideration. A young puppy will bite, mouth and jump; not because it is aggressive but because that is what puppies do.

"An adolescent dog will go through a 'teenage' phase when he will need consistent training to keep him within bounds. Most adolescent dogs will test their owner's patience. Expect this to be doubly difficult if you have small children exciting the dog.

"If you decide that the time is right to introduce a dog to your family, give careful consideration to which breed will suit you. Labradoodles are large, intelligent, bouncy dogs. Do you have the time to devote to a dog that requires a large amount of exercise and mental stimulation?

"Dogs can find children very exciting and your children will need to be taught how to behave around dogs so that accidents are not caused by the dog becoming unruly and over stimulated.

"Your dog will need a quite place of his own where he can rest, away from the children. If he has a crate, then children should be taught that they must leave him in peace when he is in his "den".
Your dog will also know that this is a safe haven when he finds the children too stressful. All interaction between dogs and children should be supervised. Excitement can quickly escalate and accidents can happen.

"An adult presence is particularly important with visiting children. House rules will need to be explained and all children will need to be shown how to behave around the dog. If you have children and dogs rampaging around the house, you may consider that it is safer and less stressful to separate the two and perhaps allow the dog some quiet time in his den.

"Teach your children never to snatch a toy from your dog and teach your dog to 'swap' on command. A dog that will willingly swap a toy for another toy or treat is less likely to start guarding his belongings. If your dog does show signs of guarding, then contact a trainer straight away before the problem escalates.

"Food time should be a relaxed affair and supervised until the dog has finished his meal. Do not leave a bowl of food on the floor, if the dog does not finish his meal then remove the bowl. If you decide to allow your dog a very high value resource such as a bone, then he should eat it in a place away from the children. You may consider that the best time for this is after they have gone to bed at night.

"For their own safety, children must be taught to respect dogs. It is unreasonable to expect any dog to tolerate taunting and teasing. If they are pushed beyond limits, they will not write a letter of complaint. All dogs can bite! "Older children will benefit from attending training classes with their dog. Many children make very good handlers and it is when a child becomes involved in training their dog that you will notice a real bond develop."

Excellent advice from the Doodle Trust; follow it and the chances of successfully integrating one lovable Doodle into your family are greatly increased. If you have reservations, why not wait until the children are a little older and more independent, when you will have extra time to devote to a dog?

The Labradoodle Coat and Colours

There are three very different coat types, and each of these coats also has variations. The three main types are:

Hair coat: also known as a flat or slick coat, although it may be straight or wavy. It is usually seen in F1 and other early generation Labradoodles. It is harsher in texture that wool or fleece and this coat often sheds, so is not normally suitable for allergy sufferers.

Fleece coat: This is the coat that most people associate with an Australian Labradoodle and is also the one that requires most maintenance. A dog with this coat must be regularly groomed to prevent matting. It should have no body odour and little to no shedding, although it is typical to find the occasional fur ball around the house. A fleece coat is acceptable for some people with allergies.

The texture should be silky and light and can range from being almost

straight, (open fleece) with just a few waves in it (wavy fleece) to coat that almost has the look of a spiral perm (curly fleece).

The Australian Labradoodle Club of America (ALAA) says: "Length is usually around five inches long. The Fleece coat texture should be light and silky quite similar to that of an Angora goat.

Appearing "to contain a silky lanolin", the fleece coat can be from loosely waved giving an almost straight appearance to deeply waved. Kemp is often found around the eyes and topline.

The absence of kemp (coarse hairs) is highly prized. Fleece coats rarely, if ever, shed. A slight shedding may occur and may be determined to the degree of wavy/curly. The less curly, the more chance of slight shedding.

"During the age of eight to 12 months, during the adolescent/maturing time you will need to groom your fleece every week. After this "transition" period, the coat will settle down and maintenance will return to normal, requiring a comb out every three to four weeks.

Wool coat: This is very dense and similar in texture to lambs' wool. It can be kept long, but that requires more grooming in this style. Kept short it is easy to maintain, has little or no doggie smell and minimal shedding. This coat is most like that of the Poodle and may be suitable for some allergy sufferers.

According to the ALAA: "The 'Ideal' wool coat should 'hang' in loose hollow spirals. Most wool coats are still exhibiting a good texture but take the appearance of a spring, not a spiral. The sprung wool coat is not desirable. A thick (dense) coat is also not desirable.

The Australian Labradoodle has a single coat. Both the Fleece and the Wool coat should naturally grow in 'staples' and be of a soft texture. Both the 'Ideal' Fleece and Wool coats spin successfully. Hair coats (hair texture that shed) are a fault and are undesirable. It is extremely rare for a wool coat to shed, and is the preferred coat type for families with severe allergies.

"To keep the wool coat long and flowing will require more maintenance. The wool coat looks beautiful cut shorter and is very easy to maintain. Grooming and a trim or clip three or four times a year is all that is required to keep the short wool coat looking great."

This is what the Australian Labradoodle Association (ALA) has to say about Australian Labradoodle coats:

- Coat length should be 4-6 inches long.
- It should be straight, wavy or forming spirals and should naturally grow in staples with a soft texture.
- It should not be too thick or dense nor should it be fluffy or fuzzy.
- It should be a single coat; any sign of a double coat is a fault.
- The ideal Fleece and Wool coats can be spun successfully.
- Hair coat [Hair texture that sheds] is undesirable and is a major fault.
- It is important that the coat gives the impression of being a fleece in type rather than dog hair.
- It is acceptable to see a coat change from the puppy to adult coat, and also during hormonal changes in fertile bitches.

Coat Colours

There are many new colours appearing. These ones are the Breed Standard of Excellence colours accepted by the ALA and ALAA:

Apricot/Gold, Red, Black, Silver and Blue – all must have black pigment

Caramel, Chocolate, Cafe, Parchment and Lavender – all must have rose pigment
Chalk (appears white but when compared to a true white it is a chalky white) – it may have rose or black pigment
Cream and Apricot Cream (all shades and combinations of cream shades are acceptable) - may have rose or black pigment

Caramel: A rich gold/apricot very much the colour of its namesake - caramel through to a deep red - must have rose pigment.

Red: A solid, even, rich red colour which should have no sprinkling of other coloured fibres throughout the coat. A true red must not be lighter at the roots than at the tips of the coat. Red can fade somewhat with age, and senior dogs showing paling of coat should not be penalised.

Apricot/Gold: The colour of a ripe apricot on the inside. A true apricot must not be lighter at the roots than at the tips of the coat. It can come in varying shades and may fade as the dog grows older. Senior dogs should not be penalised for paling of coat colour.

Blue: A dark to medium smoky blue. Blue also belongs to the Rare Colour Group. Blue dogs are born black but will have blue skin and undertonings at a young age. Any other colour throughout the blue is undesirable.

Silver: Born black but will have more of a grey skin and will develop individual silver fibres at a young age. Silver dogs can take up to 3 years to colour out and become a beautiful smoky grey through to a light iridescent platinum and varying shades in between at adulthood. Uneven layering of colour in the silver is normal.

Chocolate: Dark and rich, born almost Black, they maintain a dark chocolate throughout their lifetime. Colour should be even. Any other colour throughout the Chocolate is highly undesirable. Chocolate belongs to the Rare Colour Group.

Café: Born milk chocolate of varying shades, and have the same gene as the silver dogs, often taking up to 3 years to fully colour out to multi shades of chocolate, silvery chocolate and silver throughout. When given plenty of time in the sunshine, they develop stunning highlights.

Lavender: A definite, even smoky lavender chocolate, giving almost pink/lilac appearance. Lavender dogs are born chocolate and can be difficult to distinguish at a young age. Any other colour throughout the lavender is highly undesirable. True lavender belongs to the Rare Colour Group.

Parchment: Born milk chocolate, will pale to a smoky creamy beige. Paling usually starts from an early age often as early as six weeks. As adults they can be mistaken for dark smoky cream from a distance. Parchment belongs to the Rare Colour Group.

There are many other colours being created by breeders around the world, including parti (another colour with white), phantom (a solid body colour with markings like a Doberman or Rottweiler), sable (a dark undercoat with light tips), blue merle (marbled effect) and blue tick (parti with small spots of colour). However, none of these are recognised by the ALA or ALAA.

Tips

- Choose a responsible breeder and ask lots of questions.
- Find out whether the Labradoodle puppies are First Generation (F1) crosses, multigens or a different cross. Are the puppies Labradoodles or Australian Labradoodles?
- Try to see both parents (of the puppy, not the breeder!) Look at their size, coat and temperament.
- Labradoodles tend to have the personality type of one or the other of their parent breeds. Read about the characteristics of the Labrador and the Poodle.
- If you have allergies, spend some time with the dog or puppy before committing.

---

2. History of the Labradoodle

The origin of the domestic dog (*Canis lupus familiaris*) began with the domestication of the grey wolf tens of thousands of years ago.

Grey Wolf

Some modern breeds can trace their origins back several hundreds of years. But in terms of a 24-hour clock, the crossbreed Labradoodle's place in canine history is similar to the arrival of the human in the history of the world – we and he landed at one minute to midnight.

The term 'Labradoodle' appeared as early as 1955. British speed record breaker Donald Campbell (who died in a water speed record attempt in 1969) actually used the term 'Labradoodle' in his autobiography in 1955.

In his book 'Into the Water Barrier', he wrote: "It was a gloomy job but we had some laughs, many at the expense of my dog, Maxie. I'd had him since he was a pup in 1949 and we call him a "Labradoodle" since he is a mixture of a Labrador and a poodle, all black with thick, curly hair."

However, it wasn't until 33 years later that a Labrador and Standard Poodle were mated with the specific aim of creating the new Labradoodle crossbreed.

The man credited with breeding the first officially-recognised Labradoodles was Wally Conron, who worked as breeding manager for the Royal Guide Dog Association of Australia in Melbourne in the 1980's. His is the fascinating story of the birth of a crossbreed which was to capture the interest of dog lovers right across the globe.

Wally Conron's story

Wally received a request from a visually-impaired woman in Hawaii called Pat Blum. She had never applied for a guide dog before because of her husband's allergy to dogs, and wrote to Wally in the hope that he might be able to help. Wally at first described her request as a *"piece of cake."* But soon he was to realise that he had been somewhat optimistic.

He had the novel idea of breeding the Labrador with the Standard Poodle. His goal was to combine the low-shedding coat of the Poodle with the gentleness and trainability of the Labrador to ultimately produce a service/guide dog suitable for people with allergies to fur and dander.

He takes up the story in his own words: "The Standard Poodle, a trainable working dog, was probably the most suitable breed, with its tightly curled coat. Although our centre bred and used Labradors, I didn't anticipate any difficulties finding a suitable Poodle.

"It turned out I was wrong: after rejecting countless Poodles with various problems, some two years and 33 disappointing trials later, I still hadn't found an appropriate dog for the job. In desperation, I decided to cross a Standard Poodle with one of our best-producing Labradors. "

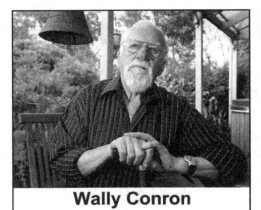
Wally Conron

He mated Brandy the Labrador with Harley, a Standard Poodle imported from Sweden. The union was successful and three pups were born: Sultan, Sheik and Simon.

Coat and saliva samples were flown to Pat in Hawaii, where it was discovered that her husband was allergic to two of the three but – Eureka! – he had no reaction to Sultan.

Wally said: "At last we were getting somewhere, but a big job lay ahead. The pup had to grow up and prove suitable for guiding work; and then it had to be compatible with the visually-impaired client. We had a long way to go."

There was a waiting list of people wanting to puppy walk for Royal Guide Dog Association of Australia, but when these new crossbreeds needed homes, no one wanted to take them in - they all preferred to wait for purebreds.

Wally knew it was important for the pups to socialise with a family, so he aired a story on Channel 9 in Melbourne about the 'new breed of guide dog'. In the show he first coined the word 'Labradoodle'.

He continued: "It worked – during the weeks that followed, our switchboard was inundated with calls from other guide dog centres, vision-impaired people and people allergic to dog hair who wanted to know more about this 'wonder dog'. My three pups may have been mongrels at heart – but the furore did not abate.

"It was 1989 and the publicity surrounding the new designer dogs went national and then international. A new world opened for countless people who had once thought they could never enjoy the delight of a pet pooch. "With this kind of response, I knew we were on to a winner, and I took the decision to breed more of the Labrador-Poodle crosses.

Pat Blum with Sultan

So I contacted the then Kennel Control Council of Australia, hoping to find the names of reputable breeders who were breeding standard problem-free Poodles.

"*'If you use any registered dog for your programme, that breeder will be struck off the register and never be allowed to show or register their dogs again,'* the council's spokesperson warned. Nor did he budge when I explained that the dogs were being bred to help vision-impaired people.

"The breeders themselves were split: many did subsequently threaten me or propose litigation if I used their progeny in my breeding programme, while others offered their services free to the guide dog centre. While all this was happening, I continued training Sultan, the original non-allergenic pup. He eventually went to Hawaii, amid intense media coverage, where as the world's first Labradoodle he bonded beautifully with his new owner and her allergic husband.

"Interest in the Labradoodle continued to escalate and inquiries poured in from all over the world from people wishing to either purchase or breed the dogs."

Sultan lived a happy life as Pat's guide dog in Hawaii for 10 years. Sheik and Simon also lived useful lives, one as a remedial dog and the other as a guide dog.

Wally quickly realised he had opened a "Pandora's Box" (as he called it) when the next litter of 10 Labradoodles produced only three allergy-free pups. In an effort to increase the ratio of allergy-friendly dogs in each litter, Wally bred Labradoodles with other Labradoodles, calling the new puppies 'Double Doodles'. Double Doodles were then bred with Double-Doodles and the offspring became 'Tri-Doodles'.

Word soon got round and when people heard about this new highly trainable and attractive crossbreed many fell in love with it. A major

25

reason was that many people believed that all Labradoodles were non-shedding and hypoallergenic (less likely to cause allergies). However, this was not true back in the 1980's and is still not true today. The nature of individual allergies varies, as does the coat of individual Labradoodles and, despite what some breeders may promise, there is no 100% guarantee.

Wally added: "I began to worry, too, about backyard breeders producing supposedly *"allergy-free"* dogs for profit. Already, one man claimed to be the first to breed a Poodle- Rottweiler cross! "Nothing, however, could stop the mania that followed. New breeds began to flood the market: groodles, spoodles, caboodles and snoodles. Were breeders bothering to check their sires and bitches for heredity faults, or were they simply caught up in delivering to hungry customers the next status symbol?"

The Labradoodle programme was ultimately abandoned by Wally, but not before 31 puppies had been bred and raised, of which 29 passed to become service dogs - although only one in 10 were reliably allergy-friendly.

In 2010 Wally, then aged 81, went on record in an interview with The Australian as saying that he regretted creating the Labradoodle. He said: "Now when people ask me: 'Did you breed the first one?' I have to say: 'Yes I did, but it's not something I'm proud of'. I wish I could turn the clock back, but the genie's out of the bottle, and you can't put it back."

Wally spoke from his home in Australia to The Associated Press in February 2014, just before the agility competition at the Westminster Dog Show, USA, which allowed mixed breed dogs to enter for the first time in its 138-year history.

He said: "I've done a lot of damage, I've created a lot of problems. Marvellous thing, my foot. There are a lot of unhealthy and abandoned dogs out there."

He told AP that he had contacted Barrack Obama: "When I heard he was thinking about a Labradoodle, I wrote to him and said to make sure he checked its pedigree."

Wally believes there are far too many unscrupulous people eager to make money at a dog's expense. He said "horrific" puppy mills are springing up and producing unstable dogs that go unwanted and eventually are euthanized.

"Instead of breeding out the problems, they're breeding them in," Wally said. "For every perfect one, you're going to find a lot of crazy ones."

The early years and controversy

The meteoric rise in popularity of the Labradoodle led to unscrupulous breeding. Without any regard to genetics, health issues or temperament, people began crossing any common-or-garden Labrador with any old Poodle - and calling the offspring 'Labradoodles'. The result was unpredictable puppies with a range of diverse physical characteristics.

Throughout those early years Kate Shoeffel, a vet in New South Wales, Australia, and others were determined to improve the Labradoodle, to fix its flaws and turn it into a highly desirable family companion. She began breeding first generation (F1) Labradoodles from purebred Labradors and Poodles and backcrossing them to Poodles (F1b). Her F1s and F1bs were amongst the first Labradoodles to be exported from Australia to America.

Ms Shoeffel founded the Australian Association of Pet Dog Breeders, but her part in this story is not without controversy. In 2013, Australian TV's 7News ran an exposé of the grim conditions for dogs at her kennels. Afterwards she said in a letter to the Australian Association of Pet Dog Breeders: "My current facility was well above current husbandry standards 18 years ago, but I am well aware it is now old and not of a standard I believe members aspire to."

In 1989, two Labradoodle breeding centres were set up by mother and daughter team Beverley Manners and Angela Wetzel Cunningham, both of whom have also recently been surrounded in controversy. The centres were Tegan Park and Rutland Manor.

The early Labrador Poodle crosses in Australia produced very large dogs, often hard-headed and hyperactive with minds of their own. They were intelligent, but with a wilful, easily-distracted nature, many of the early dogs did not make good family pets and ended up in rescue centres or, even worse, being put down (euthanized)

Although more consistency was being achieved in the allergy-friendly non-shedding coat, the headstrong, over-active temperament still remained in many offspring. If the crossbreed was to achieve Wally Conron's vision of a healthy animal suitable as a therapy and service dog and an excellent family dog for allergy sufferers, this needed to be addressed.

It was then that the idea of introducing of another pure breed was first mooted. This would widen the gene pool and, with the right choice, reduce the chances of introducing new diseases. After much research, two Irish Water Spaniels were used in some bloodlines (like the one pictured, right). The breed was chosen as it has very few congenital (birth) and genetic (inherited) diseases. Its character and temperament were also in line with the desired attributes for the Australian Labradoodle.

When several generations of selective breeding the smallest Australian Labradoodles with other very small Australian Labradoodles failed to produce consistently sized puppies - even within the same litter - it was decided to introduce English and American Cocker Spaniels. This gave the Labradoodle a larger bone structure than the smaller Poodles and introduced the Cocker Spaniel's soft fleece coat. (The Curly Coated Retriever was also used, but these lines did not work out.)

A highly successful and somewhat misguided marketing campaign by Beverley Manners and Angela Wetzel Cunningham took the world – and the USA in particular - by storm, causing 'Doodle Fever'. The demand for Labradoodles increased dramatically overnight. Suddenly everyone and anyone who could get their hands on a Standard Poodle and Labrador went into the Labradoodle breeding business.

In the late 1990s, responsible breeders who carefully selected their breeding dogs and who promoted health testing joined together. They formed the first association to protect the qualities of the multigeneration Labradoodle: the Labradoodle Association of Australia (LAA), which has since merged.

Protecting the Labradoodle legacy today

There are three main international Labradoodle organisations: the Australian Labradoodle Association of America (ALAA), The Australian

Labradoodle Association (ALA) and the Australian Labradoodle Club of America (ALCA)

ALAA, formed in 2004, manages the largest database of both Labradoodles and Australian Labradoodles in the world, with vital statistics for nearly 20,000 dogs registered by the end of 2013 and ancestral information for more than 25,000.

The organisation promotes responsible dog companionship by providing

helpful information about the breeds. Its website also serves as a resource for prospective breeders and pet owners, with a variety of information about Labradoodle traits, best practices and dog care.

ALA is working towards getting the Australian Labradoodle recognised as a pure breed (pedigree). The Association's mission statement says: "The vision of the ALA is to protect and nurture the Australian Labradoodle throughout Australia and the world for successive generations.

"To work with the Australian National Kennel Club (ANKC) towards the goal of the full recognition of the Labradoodle as a pure breed.

"To advise and guide prospective and current Labradoodle owners and breeders in order to promote the gathering together of enthusiasts for the common good of the Labradoodle breed and its fanciers.

"To maintain as far as is possible the current state of robust health in the Labradoodle."

ACLA was set up in 2005 as a non-profit organisation serving the breeders, owners and enthusiasts of the 'original' Australian Labradoodle. It states: "ALCA certifies only the original Australian Labradoodle, allowing only one Poodle infusion within three generations and does not allow any Wheaton Terrier infusion nor recognize any name other than Australian Labradoodle."

There is also the **UK Labradoodle Association,** a voluntary, informal and independent resource for anyone interested in Labradoodles in the UK. It provides information and listings for owners, prospective owners and for breeders, as well as a forum to discuss topics related to Doodles. The website states that it is "**not** run by breeders nor does it seek to dictate what is or is not best practice (though there is a published Code of Practice with which breeders listed here must comply), rather to air the options in a constructive way and let *you* decide."

The Doodle Trust, formerly the Labradoodle Trust in the UK, is an excellent source of unbiased information for prospective owners. Run by volunteers, the Trust also rehomes unwanted Doodles. The website is at www.labradoodle.com and is scheduled to move to www.doodletrust.com some time in 2014.

3. Puppies

Are You Ready?

Apart from having a baby, getting a puppy is one of the most important, demanding, expensive and life-enriching decisions you will ever make. Just like babies, puppies will love you unconditionally - but there is a price to pay. In return for their loyalty and devotion, you have to fulfil your part of the bargain.

You have to be prepared to devote several hours a day to your new Labradoodle puppy, especially in the beginning. You have to feed, exercise and train them every day as well as take care of their health and welfare. You have also to be prepared to part with hard cash for regular healthcare and even more money in veterinary bills if they fall ill. If you are not prepared, or unable, to devote the time and money to a new arrival – or if you are out at work all day – then now might not be the right time for you to consider getting a puppy.

Labradoodles, more than most dogs, are sociable creatures and generally love being with people and other dogs. To leave a Labradoodle, whether Standard, Medium or Miniature, on his own all day long is not fair on this naturally affectionate dog who enjoys being with others and involved in family life.

 As with all dogs, some may become badly behaved or even destructive if they are left alone too long. Labradoodles are intelligent dogs that are very trainable, but they need plenty of mental and physical stimulation to keep them occupied. They often want nothing more than to please their owners, but if left on their own for long periods, they may find their own entertainment – and that may be destructive.

We even know of one Standard Labradoodle who chewed a plaster wall in the passage where she was made to sleep at night, separated from her beloved owners. She kept on chewing until she had made a hole right through to the bathroom!

If you are out at work all day these are NOT the dogs for you due to their sociable nature - not even Minis. Standard Labradoodles in particular can be boisterous and mischievous if not stimulated or exercised sufficiently. If you are determined to have a dog even if you are out at work all day, then consider getting a breed which is not so emotionally dependent on humans and survives better without as much attention. Labradoodles thrive on interaction and being involved.

Labradoodles – particularly smaller ones - may live to be well into their teens, so getting a puppy is definitely a long-term commitment. Before getting a puppy, ask yourself some questions:

Have I Got Enough Time?
In the first days after leaving his or her mother and littermates, your puppy will feel very lonely and probably even a little afraid. You and your family will have to spend time with your new arrival to make him or her feel safe and sound. For the first few days, you will be around all of the time to help your puppy settle into his new home and to start bonding

with him. Book time off work if necessary, but don't just get a puppy and leave him or her alone in the house a couple of days later.

After that you will need to spend time house-training and then good behaviour training. You'll have to make time every day (no matter what the weather) for exercise. This is important, as many behaviour

problems are a result of a dog having too much energy and intelligence and not enough exercise or stimulation.

You'll also have to feed your dog daily, in fact several times a day with a young puppy. He or she will also require regular grooming. Some Labradoodles don't shed hair, but all need regular brushing to stop their hair from matting. Don't forget you will also need to take time to visit the veterinary for regular healthcare visits, such as annual inoculations.

How Long Can I Leave Him For?
This is a question we get asked all of the time on our website and one which causes a lot of debate among owners and prospective owners. Some Labradoodles have been described as "Velcro" dogs, as they like to stick to their owner. It's not unusual for them to follow you from room to room, especially at the beginning.

Labradoodles are very sociable dogs and often do well with other Labradoodles, which is why some owners have more than one.

All dogs are pack animals. Their natural state is to be with others. Being alone is not natural for a dog, although many have to get used to it.

So how many hours can you leave a dog alone for? Well, a useful guide comes from the rescue organisations. In the UK, they will not allow anybody to adopt a dog if they are intending leaving that dog alone for more than four or five hours a day.

Dogs left at home alone all day become bored and, in the case of Labradoodles and other breeds which are highly dependent on company for their happiness, may well become sad or depressed. Some of it will, of course, depend on the character and temperament of your dog. But a lonely Labradoodle may display signs of unhappiness by making a mess in the house, being destructive, behaving badly when you return or barking all of the time. Others may adapt better to being left alone.

We do not recommend leaving a Labradoodle alone for longer than five hours maximum. Even Standard Labradoodles have smaller bladders than humans. Forget the emotional side for a moment, how would you like to be left for eight hours without being able to visit the bathroom?

A puppy or fully-grown dog must NEVER be left shut in a crate all day. It is OK to leave a puppy or adult dog in a crate if they are happy there, but the door should never be closed for more than two or three hours. A crate is a place where a puppy or adult should feel safe, not a prison.

Ask yourself why you want a dog – is it for selfish reasons or can you really offer a good home to a young puppy and then adult dog for the next decade and more? Would it be more sensible to wait until you are at home more?

Is My Home Suitable?

If you have decided to get a puppy, then choose one which will fit in with your living conditions. If you live in a small apartment on the 10th floor of a high rise block, then a Standard Labradoodle would not be a good choice. They love bounding around and are happiest with lots of exercise and entertainment.

If your home is small, then of all three types of Labradoodle, a Miniature would be most suitable. Also, if you have less time to devote to your dog, a Mini would be a better choice than a Medium or Standard, which will certainly need more exercise.

Family and Neighbours

What about the other members of your family, do they all want the puppy as well? A puppy will grow into a dog which will become a part of your family for many years to come. If you have children, they will, of course, be delighted.

Make sure your puppy gets enough time to sleep – which is most of the time in the beginning. He doesn't want to be constantly pestered by young children. Sleep is very important to puppies, just as it is for babies. One of the reasons some Labradoodles end up in rescue centres is that the owners are unable to cope with the demands of small children AND a dog.

Remember that dogs are very hierarchical, in other words, there is pecking order. There is always one person that the puppy will regard as pack leader, usually the person who feeds him or who spends most time with him.

Puppies will often regard children as being on their own level, like a playmate, and so they might chase, jump and nip at them with sharp teeth. This is not aggression; this is normal play for puppies. Be sure to supervise play time and make sure the puppy does not get too boisterous.

What about the neighbours? You may think that it is none of their business, but if your dog is out in the garden or yard barking his head off all day, you can be sure they will have something to say about it. One way to prevent this is to make sure your dog gets plenty of daily exercise, so he'll be too tired to bark all day.

Older People

If you are older or have elderly relatives living with you, the good news is that Labradoodles are very sociable pets and great company. They love to be involved with people and generally have affectionate temperaments.

Bear in mind that larger dogs may be too difficult to handle for a senior citizen, especially if they haven't been trained not to jump up at people, or if they pull on the lead. If you are older, make sure your energy levels are up to those of a young puppy. Ask yourself if you are fit enough to take your dog for at least one walk every day.

My father is in his early 80's but takes Max, our dog, out for over an hour every day – even in the rain or snow. It's good for him and it's good for Max, helping to keep both of them fit and socialised! They get fresh air, exercise and the chance to communicate with other dog walkers and their pets.

Some smaller Labradoodles may survive well enough by only going out into the garden or yard, but there is really no substitute in a dog's mind for a good walk away from the home at least once a day – more with a larger dog. Just get out the lead and see how your dog reacts, you'll soon find out if he'd rather go for a walk or stay at home.

Many older people get a puppy after losing a loved one (a husband, wife or previous much-loved dog). A dog gives them something to care for and love, as well as a constant companion. Some find that smaller Labradoodles in particular make excellent companion dogs.

Single People
Many single adults own dogs, but if you live alone, having a puppy will require a lot of dedication from you. There will be nobody to share the

tasks of daily exercise, grooming and training, so taking on a dog requires a huge commitment and a lot of your time if the dog is to have a decent life.

If you are out of the house all day as well, it is not really fair to get a puppy, or even an adult dog. Left alone all day, they will feel isolated and sad. However, if you work from home, nearby or are at home all day and you can spend considerable time with the puppy every day, then great! All three types of Labradoodles make wonderful companions.

Labradoodles are known for becoming excellent family pets. Deciding on which size to get depends on factors such as the time you have available, the size of your house and garden and your energy levels. The bigger the dog, the more exercise and space they will need. Whatever the size, all Labradoodles demand a certain amount of your time and attention every day.

Other Pets

If you already have other pets in your household, spend time to introduce them gradually to each other. If you have other dogs, supervised sessions from an early age will help the dogs to get along and chances are they will become the best of friends.

Cats may be more of a problem; most dogs' natural instinct is to chase a cat. Some Labradoodles have been bred from working Labradors and they can have strong hunting instincts. It may take some a long time (if ever) to get accustomed to small pets. Others will have no problem at all.

The fact that a dog has lived with one cat will not guarantee that it will tolerate a different, strange cat. A lot will depend on the temperament of the individual dog and at what age he is introduced to the other animal(s).

Your chances of success are greater if your cat is strong-willed and your dog is docile! If your cat is timid and your dog is alert, young and active, your job will be more difficult. Supervised sessions and patience are the answer, many Labradoodles live quite happily with cats and other small animals

If a cat is already in the house, a pup may tease the cat, but in the end will probably learn to live with it. It is much harder to get an adult Labradoodle to get used to cats or other animals in the house, especially if he has been used to chasing cats, squirrels, birds and generally any creature smaller than himself on his daily walks.

Take the process slowly. If your cat is stressed and frightened, he may decide to leave. Our feline friends are notorious for abandoning home because the food and facilities are better down the road. Until you know that they can get on together, don't leave them alone.

For a dog to get on with a cat,

you are asking him to forget his natural instincts and to respond to your training. But do not despair, it can be done very successfully with Labradoodles.

If you're still determined to have a Labradoodle when you are out all day, or for several hours at a time, here are some useful points:

Top 10 Tips For Working Labradoodle Owners

1. Either come home during your lunch break to let your dog out or employ a dog walker (or neighbour) to take him out for a walk in the middle of the day.

2. Do you know anybody you could leave your dog with during the day? Consider leaving the dog with a relative or elderly neighbour who would welcome the companionship of a dog without the full responsibility of ownership.

3. Take him for as long a walk as possible before you go to work – even if this means getting up at the crack of dawn – and walk him as soon as you get home.

Exercise generates serotonin in the brain and has a calming effect. A dog that has had a good run for half an hour before you leave home will be less anxious and more ready for a good nap.

4. Leave him in a place of his own where he feels comfortable. If you use a crate, leave the door open, otherwise his favourite dog bed or basket. If possible, leave him in a room with a view of the outside world. This will be more interesting than staring at four blank walls.

5. Make sure there are no cold draughts– or that it won't get too hot during the day.

6. Food and drink: remove his food and put it down at specific meal times. If the food is there all day, he may become a fussy eater or 'punish' you for leaving him alone by refusing to eat. He needs access to water at all times. Dogs cannot cool down by sweating; they do not have many sweat glands (which is why they pant, but this is much less efficient than perspiring) and can die without sufficient water.

7. Leave toys available for him to play with. Stuff a Kong toy with his favourite to keep him occupied for a while.

Choose the right size of Kong for your dog and then put a treat inside. You can smear the inside with peanut butter or another treat to keep him occupied for longer.

8. Have you got a fenced-in garden or yard? Can you fit a dog flap to one of your doors to allow your Labradoodle to go in and out of the house during the day? You can buy door flaps which respond to an electronic signal on your dog's collar so that only he is allowed in and out of the house.

If you do use a dog flap, your garden should be dog-proof so he can't wander off. However, it may not be advisable to fit one if your garden is visible from the street. Labradoodles are very handsome and there's always a risk of them being dognapped; the theft of valuable dogs seems to be on the increase.

9. Consider leaving a radio or TV on very softly in the background. The 'white noise' can have a soothing effect on some pets. If you do this, select your channel carefully – try and avoid one with lots of bangs and crashes or heavy metal music!

10. Stick to the same routine before you leave your dog home alone. This will help him feel secure. Before you go to work, get into a daily habit for getting yourself ready, then feeding and exercising your Labradoodle. Dogs love routine.

You could consider getting two dogs to keep each other company while you are out. But remember, this will involve even more of your time and twice the expense.

And finally, when you come home your Labradoodle will be ecstatically pleased to see you. Greet him normally, but try not to go overboard by making too much of a fuss of him as soon as you walk through the door.

Give him a pat and a stroke then take off your coat and do a few other things before turning your attention back to him. Lavishing your Labradoodle with too much attention the second you walk through the door may encourage separation anxiety or demanding behaviour.

Puppy Stages

It is important to understand how a puppy develops into a fully grown dog. This knowledge will help you to be a good guardian to your puppy. The first few months and weeks will have an effect on your pup's behaviour and temperament for the rest of his life. This Puppy Schedule will help you to understand the early stages:

Birth to seven weeks	A puppy needs sleep, food and warmth. He needs his mother for security and discipline and littermates for learning and socialisation. The puppy learns to function within a pack and learns the pack order of dominance. He begins to become aware of his environment. During this period, puppies should be left with their mother.
Eight to 12 weeks	A puppy should not leave his mother before eight weeks. At this age the brain is fully developed and he now needs socialising with the outside world. He needs to change from being part of a canine pack to being part of a human pack. This period is a fear period for the puppy, avoid causing him fright and pain.
13 to 16 weeks	Training and formal obedience should begin. He needs socialising with other humans, places and situations. This period will pass easily if you remember that this is a puppy's change to adolescence. Be firm and fair. His flight instinct may be prominent. Avoid being too strict or too soft with him during this time and praise his good behaviour.
Four to eight months	Another fear period for a puppy is between seven to eight months of age. It passes quickly, but be cautious of fright or pain which may leave the puppy traumatised. The puppy reaches sexual maturity and dominant traits are established. Your dog should now understand the commands 'sit', 'down', 'come' and 'stay'.

Plan Ahead

Puppies usually leave the litter for their new homes when they are eight weeks or older. Toy breeds may stay with the mother for up to 12 weeks. Like all dogs, Labradoodle puppies learn the rules of the pack from their mothers. Most continue teaching their pups the correct manners and dos and don'ts until they are around eight weeks old.

Breeders who allow their pups to leave before this time may be more interested in a quick buck than a long-term puppy placement. Top breeders often have waiting lists. If you want a well-bred Labradoodle puppy, it pays to plan ahead.

If you have decided you are definitely going to get a puppy, and you know which size of Labradoodle will fit in best with you and your family, then the next step is probably the most important decisions you will make: **choosing the right breeder**.

Like you, your Labradoodle puppy will be a product of his or her parents and will inherit many of their characteristics. His temperament and how healthy your puppy will be now and throughout his life will largely depend on the genes of his parents.

It is essential that you select a good, responsible breeder. They will have checked out the temperament and health records of the parents and will only breed from suitable stock. There are many Labradoodle breeders on the internet and many are trustworthy and conscientious.

However, with the cost of a Labradoodle puppy rising in some cases to four-figure sums, there are also many unscrupulous breeders out there who have been tempted by the prospect of making a quick buck. Make no mistake, with many Labradoodle pups fetching four-figure sums, breeding several litters a year is a commercial business.

We would strongly recommend visiting the breeder rather than buying unseen online. There is so much variation with Labradoodles in terms of looks, coat, size and whether they are more or less likely to cause allergies, you really should follow our guidelines, visit the breeder and ask all the right questions before making this massive decision. This is an absolute MUST for allergy sufferers, as allergic reactions can vary from one dog to another – even within the same litter.

Putting a puppy through the trauma of being shipped across states or even internationally should only be done in very special circumstances.

We'd also recommend following our **Top 10 Tips for Selecting a Good Breeder**. Buying a less expensive or unseen puppy may save you money or hassle in the short term, but could cost you a fortune in extra veterinary bills or dog training lessons in the long run, not to mention the heartache of having a sickly dog.

Rescue groups know only too well the dangers of buying a poorly-bred dog. Many years of problems – with either health or behaviour – can follow, causing pain and distress for both dog and owner. All rescue groups strongly recommend taking the time to find a good breeder.

There are lots of good Labradoodle breeders who have the right puppy for you - but how do you find them? Everybody knows you should get your puppy from "a good breeder." But how can you tell the good guys from the bad guys? If you were looking for a pedigree (purebred), the Kennel Club in your country would be a good place to start, as they have lists of approved breeders. However, as the Labradoodle is a crossbreed, there are no Kennel Club lists.

You might have had a personal recommendation, or like the look of a friend's cute Labradoodle and want to have one which looks the same. If that's the case, make sure you ask all the right questions of the breeder about how they select their breeding stock and ask to see the parents' certificates for hips, elbows and eyes (the puppy's, not the breeder's!)

Another good place to start looking is the breed association in your country. These organisations all have a list of accredited breeders:
UK : the UK Labradoodle Association www.labradoodle.org.uk
 UK Australian Labradoodle Club Association
www.ukaustralianlabradoodleclub.co.uk **USA**: Australian Labradoodle Association of America http://alaa-labradoodles.com
Australian Labradoodle Club of America
www.australianlabradoodleclub.us
 Australia: the Australian Labradoodle Association lists hundreds of breeders worldwide at www.laa.org.au

If the breeder you are thinking of using is not listed by one of these associations, ask yourself – and the breeder - why not? This is what the UK Australian Labradoodle Club Association says:

"We aim to help you seek reputable Australian Labradoodle Breeders, with sound credentials, who carry out all the necessary health testings on all their breeding stock, care and love their dogs <u>as well as</u> breeding with integrity and from Australian Labradoodles with wonderful character and temperament."

"**The breeders and their Health Certificates are thoroughly checked and it is their <u>DOGS</u> that receive Accreditation based on the Health Testings performed on Breeding Stock, rather than the Breeder themselves. UK Australian Labradoodle Club Member Breeders will be able to supply you with a pedigree for your puppy which will clearly state whether your puppy is 100% ASD or an Australian Labradoodle with broken lines.**"

If you're not able to buy a puppy from one of these accredited breeders and you've never bought a Labradoodle puppy before, how do you avoid buying one from a "backstreet breeder" or puppy mill? These are people who just breed puppies for profit and sell them to the first person who turns up with the cash. Unhappily, as Wally Conron (the man who bred the first Labradoodles) was all too aware, this can end in heartbreak for a family months or years later when their puppy develops health problems due to poor breeding.

Good Labradoodle breeders will only breed from dogs which have been carefully selected for size, temperament, health and lineage and possibly coat. There are plenty out there, it's just a question of finding one. There are signs that can help the savvy buyer identify a good breeder.

Top 10 Tips for Selecting a Good Breeder

1. They keep the dogs in the home and as part of the family - not outside in kennel runs. You should also make sure the area where the puppies are kept is clean.

2. They have Labradoodles which appear happy and healthy. The dogs are excited to meet new people, and don't shy away from visitors.

3. A good dog breeder will encourage you to spend time with the puppy's parents - or at least the pup's mother - when you visit. They want your entire family to meet the puppy and are happy for you to make more than one visit.

4. They breed only one or maximum two types of dogs and they are very familiar with the 'breed standards,' even though the Labradoodle is a crossbreed. See our information on **Breed Standards** to find out exactly how Labradoodles should look.

5. Like purebreds, Labradoodles can have potential genetic weaknesses. A good breeder should explain these and should have documents to prove that both parents are free from any genetic defects such as hip dysplasia,

elbow dysplasia and eye problems like progressive retinal atrophy (PRA) and hereditary cataracts.

6. Responsible breeders should provide you with a contract and health guarantee and allow you plenty of time to read it. They will also show you records of the puppy's veterinary visits and explain what vaccinations he will need.

7. They give you guidance on caring and training for your puppy and are available for your assistance after you take your puppy home.

8. They feed their dogs high quality dog food.

9. They don't always have puppies available, but will keep a list of interested people for the next available litter.

10. And finally... good Labradoodle breeders will provide references of other families who have bought their puppies. Make sure you call at least one.

A good breeder will also agree to take a puppy back within a certain time frame if it does not work out for you, or if there is a health problem. Happy, healthy puppies are what everybody wants. Taking the time now to find a responsible Labradoodle breeder is time well spent. It could save you a lot of time, money and worry in the future and help to ensure that you and your chosen puppy are happy together for many years.

Labradoodle Litter Size

The question "How big is a Labradoodle litter?" is not an easy one to answer. Depending on which type and size of Labradoodle you are getting, litter size will vary. In very general terms, an average litter size might be around eight puppies, but it can vary from anything from four to 15.

---

10 Questions to Ask a Breeder

1. Have the parents been health screened? Ask to see original copies of hip, elbow and eye certificates.

2. Can you put me in touch with someone who already has one of your puppies? Follow up recommendations.

3. Are you a member of one of the Labradoodle associations or clubs, and are you listed as a recommended breeder?

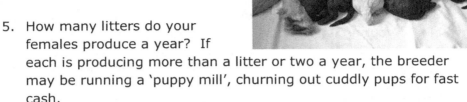

4. How long have you been breeding Labradoodles? (You are looking for someone who has a proven track record).

5. How many litters do your females produce a year? If each is producing more than a litter or two a year, the breeder may be running a 'puppy mill', churning out cuddly pups for fast cash.

6. Do you breed any other types of dog? It's a good idea to buy your puppy from a Labradoodle specialist; someone who breeds several types of dog may be more interested in the income than improving the (cross)breed.

7. What is so special about this litter of puppies? You are looking for a breeder who has used good breeding stock and his or her knowledge of the cross breed to produce **healthy dogs with good temperaments** suited to family life, not just a dog which looks cute. You may also be looking for one which is low-shedding and more allergy-friendly. There has not been a Labradoodle pup born who wasn't gorgeous! Don't buy the first one you see – be patient and pick the right one. If you don't get a satisfactory answer, consider looking elsewhere.

8. What do you feed your adults and puppies? Look for a quality dog food.

9. How big will my puppy grow? The answer will depend on whether your puppy is an F1 or multigeneration Labradoodle, but an experienced breeder with proven stock should be able to give you a good idea of how big the adult dog will be.

10. If there is a health or temperament issue with the puppy, what guarantees do I have that I can return him or her? Check whether you will have a verbal guarantee or a written contract – the latter is always better.

One question not to ask: Will my Labradoodle shed hair? Many breeders promise that their little darlings will not shed, but there is no such thing as a 100% non-shedding dog – not even a pure bred (pedigree). You can ask about the amount of shedding and with many Labradoodles this is minimal. Read what the Kennel Clubs have to say on it in **Chapter 4. Labradoodles for Allergy Sufferers.**

Top 12 Tips for Selecting a Healthy Puppy

1. Labradoodles are generally robust dogs and your puppy should have a well-fed appearance. They should NOT, however, have a distended abdomen (pot belly) as this can be a sign of worms (or Cushing's Disease in adults).

2. The ideal Labradoodle puppy should not be too thin either. You should not be able to see his ribs.

3. The puppy's eyes should be bright and clear with no mucus or discharge.

4. His nose should be cool, damp and clean with no discharge.

5. The pup's ears should also be clean and again there should be no discharge or dirty build-up.

6. His gums should be clean and a healthy pink colour.

7. Check his bottom to make sure it is clean and there are no signs of diarrhoea.

8. A Labradoodle's coat, of whatever type, should be clean with no signs of ticks or fleas. Red or irritated skin or bald spots could be a sign of infestation or a skin condition

9. The puppy should breathe normally with no coughing or wheezing.

10. When the puppy is distracted, clap or make a noise behind him (not too loud) to make sure he's not deaf.

11. Choose a puppy that is solid in build and moves well without any sign of injury or lameness.

12. Finally, ask to see veterinary records confirming he has been wormed and had his first vaccinations.

If you are unlucky enough to have a health problem with your puppy within the first few months, a reputable breeder will allow you to return the pup. However, this can be a heart-wrenching decision if you have bonded with the pup, far better to spend the time selecting from healthy, accredited stock. But if you do get your Labradoodle puppy home and things don't work out for whatever reason, good breeders should also take him back. Make sure this is the case before you commit.

Choosing the Right Temperament

If you've decided that a Labradoodle is the ideal dog for you, then here are two important points to bear in mind at the outset:

Find a responsible breeder with a good reputation (this cannot be stressed strongly enough). Secondly, take your time. Choosing a puppy which will share your home and your life for the next 10 to 15 years is a big decision. Don't rush it.

You've probably opted for a Doodle because you like the look of the dogs and their temperament, or you might want a low or non-shedding dog. Presumably you're planning on spending a lot of time with your new puppy, as Labradoodles are people dogs. If you've chosen a Standard, then be prepared for lots of daily exercise as well.

Individuals

The next thing to remember is that while different Labradoodles may share many characteristics and temperament traits, each puppy also has his own individual character, just like humans.

Are you fit and active - do you want a lively, energetic dog? Or are you older and maybe live alone? If so, a smaller, more placid Labradoodle will suit you better, or maybe an older dog which needs re-homing. If possible, visit the breeder's more than once to get an idea of your chosen pup's character in comparison to his or her littermates.

Some Labradoodle puppies will run up to greet you, pull at your shoelaces and playfully bite your fingers. Others will be more content to stay in the basket sleeping. Watch their behaviour and energy levels. Which puppy will be suitable?

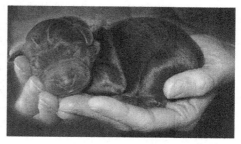

Submissive or Dominant?

A submissive dog will by nature be more passive, less energetic and also possibly easier to train. A dominant dog will usually be more energetic and lively. They may also need a firmer hand when training or socialising with other dogs.

There is no good or bad, it's a question of which type of character best suits you and your lifestyle. Here are a couple of quick tests to try at the breeder's to see if your puppy has a submissive or dominant personality:

* Roll the Labradoodle puppy gently on to his or her back in the crook of your arm (or on the floor). Then rest a hand on the pup's chest and look into his eyes for a few seconds. If he immediately struggles to get free, he is considered to be **dominant**.
A puppy that doesn't struggle, but is happy to stay on his or her back has a more **submissive** character.

* A similar test is the suspension test. Gently lift the puppy at arm's length under the armpits for a few seconds while allowing his hind legs to dangle free. A dominant pup will kick and struggle to get free. A puppy that is happy to remain dangling is more submissive.

Useful Tips

Here are some other useful signs to look out for –
* Watch how he interacts with his littermates. Does he try and dominate them, does he walk away from them or is he happy to play with them? This may give you an idea of how easy it will be to socialize him with other dogs.
* After having contact with the puppy, does he want to follow you or walk away from you? Not following may mean he has a more independent nature.
* If you throw something for the puppy is he happy to retrieve it for you or does he ignore it? This may measure their willingness to work with humans.

Decide which type of temperament would fit in with you and your family and the rest is up to you. A Labradoodle that has constant positive interactions with people and other animals during the first three to four months of life will be a more stable, happier dog.

In contrast, a puppy plucked from its family and isolated at home alone for weeks on end will be less happy, less socialised and may well have behaviour problems later on. Puppies are like children. Being properly raised contributes to their confidence, sociability, stability and intellectual development.

The bottom line is that a pup raised in a warm, loving environment with people is likely to be more tolerant and accepting and less likely to develop problems. For those who prefer a scientific approach to choosing the right puppy, we include the full *Volhard Puppy Aptitude Test.*

This has been developed by the highly respected Wendy and Jack Volhard who have built up an international reputation over the last 30 years for their invaluable contribution to dog training, health and nutrition.

 They have written eight books and the Volhard PAT is regarded as the premier method for evaluating the nature of young puppies. Jack and Wendy have also written the excellent Dog **Training for Dummies** book. Visit their website at www.volhard.com for details of their upcoming Dog Training Camps, as well as their training and nutrition groups.

The Volhard Puppy Aptitude Test

Here are the ground rules for performing the test:

- The testing is done in a location unfamiliar to the puppies. This does not mean they have to taken away from home. A 10-foot square area is perfectly adequate, such as a room in the house where the puppies have not been.

- The puppies are tested one at a time.

- There are no other dogs or people, except the scorer and the tester, in the testing area

- The puppies do not know the tester.

- The scorer is a disinterested third party and not the person interested in selling you a puppy.

- The scorer is unobtrusive and positions himself so he can observe the puppies' responses without having to move.

- The puppies are tested before they are fed.

- The puppies are tested when they are at their liveliest.

- Do not try to test a puppy that is not feeling well.

- Puppies should not be tested the day of or the day after being vaccinated.

Only the first response counts! *Tip: During the test, watch the puppy's tail. It will make a difference in the scoring whether the tail is up or down.*

The tests are simple to perform and anyone with some common sense can do them. You can, however, elicit the help of someone who has tested puppies before and knows what they are doing.

Social attraction - the owner or caretaker of the puppies places it in the test area about four feet from the tester and then leaves the test area. The tester kneels down and coaxes the puppy to come to him or her by encouragingly and gently clapping hands and calling. The tester must coax the puppy in the opposite direction from where it entered the test area. Hint: Lean backward, sitting on your heels instead of leaning forward toward the puppy. Keep your hands close to your body encouraging the puppy to come to you instead of trying to reach for the puppy.

Following - the tester stands up and slowly walks away encouraging the puppy to follow. Hint: Make sure the puppy sees you walk away and get

the puppy to focus on you by lightly clapping your hands and using verbal encouragement to get the puppy to follow you. Do not lean over the puppy.

Restraint - the tester crouches down and gently rolls the puppy on its back for 30 seconds. Hint: Hold the puppy down without applying too much pressure. The object is not to keep it on its back but to test its response to being placed in that position.

Social Dominance - let the puppy stand up or sit and gently stroke it from the head to the back while you crouch beside it. See if it will lick your face, an indication of a forgiving nature. Continue stroking until you see a behaviour you can score. Hint: When you crouch next to the puppy avoid leaning or hovering over it. Have the puppy at your side, both of you facing in the same direction.

Tip: During testing maintain a positive, upbeat and friendly attitude toward the puppies. Try to get each puppy to interact with you to bring out the best in him or her. Make the test a pleasant experience for the puppy.

Elevation Dominance - the tester cradles the puppy with both hands, supporting the puppy under its chest and gently lifts it two feet off the ground and holds it there for 30 seconds.

Retrieving - the tester crouches beside the puppy and attracts its attention with a crumpled up piece of paper. When the puppy shows some interest, the tester throws the paper no more than four feet in front of the puppy encouraging it to retrieve the paper.

Touch Sensitivity - the tester locates the webbing of one the puppy's front paws and presses it lightly between his index finger and thumb. The tester gradually increases pressure while counting to ten and stops when the puppy pulls away or shows signs of discomfort.

Sound Sensitivity - the puppy is placed in the centre of the testing area and an assistant stationed at the perimeter makes a sharp noise, such as banging a metal spoon on the bottom of a metal pan.

Sight Sensitivity - the puppy is placed in the centre of the testing area. The tester ties a string around a bath towel and jerks it across the floor, two feet away from the puppy.

Stability - an umbrella is opened about five feet from the puppy and gently placed on the ground. During the testing, make a note of the heart rate of the pup, this is an indication of how it deals with stress, as well as its energy level.

Puppies come with high, medium or low energy levels. You have to decide for yourself, which suits your life style. Dogs with high energy levels need a great deal of exercise, and will get into mischief if this energy is not channelled into the right direction.

Finally, look at the overall structure of the puppy. You see what you get at 49 days age (seven weeks). If the pup has strong and straight front and back legs, with all four feet pointing in the same direction, it will grow up that way, provided you give it the proper diet and environment. If you notice something out of the ordinary at this age, it will stay with puppy for the rest of its life. He will not grow out of it.

Scoring the Results

Following are the responses you will see and the score assigned to each particular response. You will see some variations and will have to make a judgment on what score to give them –

Test	Response	Score
SOCIAL ATTRACTION	Came readily, tail up, jumped, bit at hands	1
	Came readily, tail up, pawed, licked at hands	2
	Came readily, tail up	3
	Came readily, tail down	4
	Came hesitantly, tail down	5
	Didn't come at all	6
FOLLOWING	Followed readily, tail up, got underfoot, bit at feet	1
	Followed readily, tail up, got underfoot	2

	Followed readily, tail up	3
	Followed readily, tail down	4
	Followed hesitantly, tail down	5
	Did not follow or went away	6
RESTRAINT	Struggled fiercely, flailed, bit	1
	Struggled fiercely, flailed	2
	Settled, struggled, settled with some eye contact	3
	Struggled, then settled	4
	No struggle	5
	No struggle, strained to avoid eye contact	6
SOCIAL DOMINANCE	Jumped, pawed, bit, growled	1
	Jumped, pawed	2
	Cuddled up to tester and tried to lick face	3
	Squirmed, licked at hands	4
	Rolled over, licked at hands	5
	Went away and stayed away	6
ELEVATION DOMINANCE	Struggled fiercely, tried to bite	1
	Struggled fiercely	2
	Struggled, settled, struggled, settled	3
	No struggle, relaxed	4
	No struggle, body stiff	5
	No struggle, froze	6
RETRIEVING	Chased object, picked it up and ran away	1
	Chased object, stood over it and did not return	2
	Chased object, picked it up and returned with it to tester	3
	Chased object and returned without it to tester	4
	Started to chase object, lost interest	5
	Does not chase object	6

TOUCH SENSITIVITY	8-10 count before response	1
	6-8 count before response	2
	5-6 count before response	3
	3-5 count before response	4
	2-3 count before response	5
	1-2 count before response	6
SOUND SENSITIVITY	Listened, located sound and ran toward it barking	1
	Listened, located sound and walked slowly toward it	2
	Listened, located sound and showed curiosity	3
	Listened and located sound	4
	Cringed, backed off and hid behind tester	5
	Ignored sound and showed no curiosity	6
SIGHT SENSITIVITY	Looked, attacked and bit object	1
	Looked and put feet on object and put mouth on it	2
	Looked with curiosity and attempted to investigate, tail up	3
	Looked with curiosity, tail down	4
	Ran away or hid behind tester	5
	Hid behind tester	6
STABILITY	Looked and ran to the umbrella, mouthing or biting it	1
	Looked and walked to the umbrella, smelling it cautiously	2
	Looked and went to investigate	3
	Sat and looked, but did not move toward the umbrella	4
	Showed little or no interest	5
	Ran away from the umbrella	6

The scores are interpreted as follows:

Mostly 1's

Strong desire to be pack leader and is not shy about bucking for a

promotion. Has a predisposition to be aggressive to people and other dogs and will bite
Should only be placed into a very experienced home where the dog will be trained and worked on a regular basis

Tip: Stay away from the puppy with a lot of 1's or 2's. It has lots of leadership aspirations and may be difficult to manage. This puppy needs an experienced home. Not good with children.

Mostly 2's
 Also has leadership aspirations
May be hard to manage and has the capacity to bite
Has lots of self-confidence
Should not be placed into an inexperienced home
Too unruly to be good with children and elderly people, or other animals
Needs strict schedule, loads of exercise and lots of training
Has the potential to be a great show dog with someone who understands dog behaviour

Mostly 3's
Can be a high-energy dog and may need lots of exercise
Good with people and other animals. Can be a bit of a handful to live with

Needs training, does very well at it and learns quickly
Great dog for second time owner.

Mostly 4's
The kind of dog that makes the perfect pet.
Best choice for the first time owner.
Rarely will buck for a promotion in the family

Easy to train, and rather quiet.
Good with elderly people, children, although may need protection from the children
Choose this pup, take it to obedience classes, and you'll be the star, without having to do too much work!
Tip: The puppy with mostly 3's and 4's can be quite a handful, but should be good with children and does well with training. Energy needs to be dispersed with plenty of exercise.

Mostly 5's
Fearful, shy and needs special handling
Will run away at the slightest stress in its life
Strange people, strange places, different floor or surfaces may upset it
Often afraid of loud noises and terrified of thunder storms. When you

greet it upon your return, may submissively urinate. Needs a very special home where the environment doesn't change too much and where there are no children. Best for a quiet, elderly couple

If cornered and cannot get away, has a tendency to bite

Tip: Avoid the puppy with several 6's. It is so independent it doesn't need you or anyone. He is his own person and unlikely to bond to you.

Mostly 6's

So independent that he doesn't need you or other people

Doesn't care if he is trained or not - he is his own person Unlikely to bond to you, since he doesn't need you.

A great guard dog for gas stations!

Do not take this puppy and think you can change him into a lovable bundle - you can't, so leave well enough alone.

The Scores

Few puppies will test with all 2's or all 3's, there'll be a mixture of scores. For that first time, wonderfully easy to train, potential star, look for a puppy that scores with mostly 4's and 3's. Don't worry about the score on Touch Sensitivity - you can compensate for that with the right training equipment.

It's hard not to become emotional when picking a puppy - they are all so cute, soft and cuddly. Remind yourself that this dog is going to be with you for eight to 16 years. Don't hesitate to step back a little to contemplate your decision. Sleep on it and review it in the light of day.

Avoid the puppy with a score of 1 on the Restraint and Elevation tests. This puppy will be too much for the first-time owner. It's a lot more fun to have a good dog, one that is easy to train, one you can live with and one you can be proud of, than one that is a constant struggle.

Getting a Dog From a Shelter

Don't overlook an Animal Shelter as a source for a good dog. Not all dogs wind up in a shelter because they are bad. After that cute puppy stage, when the dog grows up, it may become too much for its owner.

Or, there has been a change in the owner's circumstances forcing him or her into having to give up the dog.

Most of the time these dogs are housetrained and already have some training. If the dog has been properly socialised to people, it will be able to adapt to a new environment. Bonding may take a little longer, but once accomplished, results in a devoted companion.

A Dog or a Bitch (Male or Female)?

When you have decided to get a Labradoodle puppy and know how to find a good breeder, the next decision is whether to get a male or female.

The differences within the sexes are greater than the differences between the sexes. In other words, you can get a dominant female and a submissive male, or vice versa. There are, however, some general traits which are more common with one sex or another.

Labradoodles are sociable dogs and, unless they have had a bad experience, they are not normally aggressive. However, un-neutered males – usually just referred to as 'dogs' – are more likely to be aggressive towards other males. That goes for all breeds and crossbreeds. Most males will not deliberately start a fight, but an un-neutered one is more likely to defend whatever he regards as his territory – and this include you!

One other thing with males is that on walks they will mark their territory by urinating many times along the way – and you can't rush them! Females will generally just empty their bladder once or twice on a walk.

An entire (un-neutered) male is also more likely to go wandering off on the scent of a female. This happened with our dog Max several times. On walks he sniffed out the trail of a bitch "on heat" (the time on her menstrual cycle when she is ready for mating). Although normally fairly obedient, our calls for him to come back fell on deaf ears – Max had other things on his mind - and disappeared over the fields.

We were lucky, he was brought back home by strangers. After the third time, we had him neutered and he has never run off since. According to Graham, our vet, Max is much more content now as he is not thinking about sex all of the time!

Female Labradoodles (bitches) generally tend to be less aggressive towards other dogs, except when they are raising puppies. You might want to consider a female if you have young children and are looking for a family companion. A bitch may be more tolerant toward young creatures, including your children. Bear in mind that when you select your puppy, you should also be looking out for the right temperament as well as the right sex.

Unless you bought your Labradoodle specifically for breeding, it is recommended you have your dog neutered, or spayed if she is a female. If you plan to have two or more Labradoodles living together, this is even more advisable.

It is generally thought that spaying and neutering may also reduce the risk of certain types of cancer and lead to a longer lifespan in some cases. But there are always two sides to every argument, see our **Chapter 12. The Birds and The Bees.**

Puppy Checklist

Here's a list of some of the things you might need before bringing your puppy home:

-A dog bed or basket
-Bedding – old towels or a blanket which can easily be washed
-If possible, a towel or piece of cloth which has been rubbed on the puppy's mother to put in his bed
-Collar and lead
-Identification tag for the puppy's collar
-Food and water bowls
-A puppy coat if you live in a cold climate
-Lots of newspapers for house training
-Poo bags
-A crate
-Some old towels for cleaning your puppy and covering the crate if you decide to use one.
-Puppy food – find out what the breeder is feeding
-Puppy treats

-Toys and chews suitable for puppies
-PLENTY OF TIME!

Later on you'll also need a larger collar, a longer lead, grooming brushes, dog shampoo and flea and worming products and maybe other items such as a harness or a travel crate.

Vaccinations

When your new puppy arrives home, you should make an appointment with your vet to complete his vaccinations if he hasn't already had them all. All puppies need these shots.

The usual schedule is for the pup to have his first vaccination at or after seven weeks old. This will protect him from a number of diseases in one

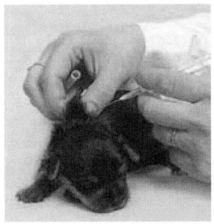

shot. These may include Canine Parvovirus (Parvo), Distemper, Infectious Canine Hepatitis (Adenvirus), Leptospirosis and Kennel Cough. In the USA, puppies may also need vaccinating separately against Rabies and Lyme Disease.

He will need a second and maybe a third vaccination a few weeks later to complete his immunity. Consult your vet to find out exactly what injections are needed for the area you live in.

Diseases such as Parvo and Kennel Cough are highly contagious and you should not let your puppy mix with other dogs - unless they are your own and have already been vaccinated - until he has completed his vaccinations, otherwise he will not be fully immunised. You also shouldn't take him to places where unvaccinated dogs might have been, like the local park.

Your dog will need a booster injection every year of his life. Your vet should give you a record card or send you a reminder, but it's a good idea to keep a note of the date in your diary.

Vaccinations are generally quite safe and side effects are uncommon. If your puppy is unlucky enough to be one of the few that does have an adverse reaction to his shots, here are the signs to look out for, a pup may have one or more of these:

Mild Reaction:
Sleepiness
Irritability and not wanting to be touched
Sore or a small lump at the place where he was injected
Nasal discharge or sneezing
Puffy face ears. and

Severe Reaction:
Anaphylactic shock. A sudden and quick reaction, usually before leaving the vet's, which causes breathing difficulties.
Vomiting
Diarrhoea
Staggering and seizures

A severe reaction is extremely rare. There is a far, far greater risk of your puppy being ill and spreading disease if he does not have the vaccinations.

Bringing a New Puppy Home

First of all, make sure that you have puppy-proofed your home. Remember that most Labradoodle puppies are nosy little chewing machines, so remove anything breakable and chewable within the puppy's reach.

You may also want to remove your precious oriental rugs and keep the pup off your expensive carpets until he is fully house-trained and has stopped chewing everything in sight. Not all puppies chew a lot, but many do.

Designate a place within your home which will be the puppy's area. An area with a wooden or tiled floor would be a good start until he or she is house-trained.

Make sure that the area is warm enough, but not too warm.
It should not take him too long to get used to his new surroundings, but the first few days will be traumatic for him and he'll probably whine a lot. Imagine a small child being taken away from his mother; that is how your Labradoodle pup will feel.

If you have a garden or a yard that you intend letting your puppy roam in, t every little gap needs plugging. You'd be amazed at the tiny holes they can escape through.

For your puppy to grow into a well-adjusted dog, he has to feel comfortable and relaxed in his new surroundings. He is leaving the warmth and protection of his mother and littermates and so for the first few days at least, your puppy will feel very sad. It is important to make the transition from the birth home to your home as easy as possible.

His life is in your hands. How you react and interact with him in the first few days and weeks will shape your relationship and his character for the years ahead.

The First Few Days
This can be a very stressful time for a Labradoodle puppy and a worrying time for new owners. Your puppy has just been taken away from his mother, brothers and sisters and is feeling very sorry for himself.

Our website receives many emails from worried new owners. Here are some of the most common concerns:

* My puppy sleeps all the time, is this normal?
* My puppy won't stop crying or whining
* My puppy is shivering
* My puppy won't eat
* My puppy is very timid
* My puppy follows me everywhere, she won't let me out of her sight

Most of the above are quite common. They are just a young pup's reaction to leaving all he knows and entering into a strange new world. It is normal for puppies to sleep most of the time. It is also normal for some to whine a lot during the first few days. Make him as comfortable as possible, ensuring he has a warm, quiet place which is his, where he is not pestered by children or other pets. Talk in a soft, reassuring voice to him and handle him gently, while giving him plenty time to sleep.

Unless they are especially dominant, most puppies will be nervous and timid for the first few days. They will think of you as their new mother and may follow you around the house. This is also quite natural, but after a few days, start to leave your puppy for a few minutes at a time, gradually building up the period away. If you are never parted, he may develop separation anxiety when you do have to leave him. (See our section on **Separation Anxiety.)**

If you will be out of the house for most of the day, try to get your puppy on a Friday or Saturday so she has at least a couple of days to adjust to her new surroundings.

A better idea is to book at least a week off work to help your puppy settle in. If you don't work, leave your diary free for the first few days. Getting a new pup and helping him settle in properly is virtually a full-time job in the beginning.

Before you collect your Doodle pup, let the breeder know when you are coming and ask for him not to be fed for three or four hours beforehand. He'll be less likely to be car sick and should be hungry when he arrives in his new surroundings.

Make sure she gets plenty of rest. If you have children, don't let them constantly waken the pup. Don't invite friends round to see your cuddly little pup for at least a day or more. However excited you are, he needs a quiet 24 hours or more.

It is a frightening time for the little chap. Talk softly and gently stroke him, he needs plenty of reassurance. If you can, bring home a piece of cloth which has been rubbed with the mother's scent and put it in his bed. Is your puppy shivering with cold or nerves? Make sure he is in a warm, safe, quiet place away from any draughts and loud noises.

If your puppy is off his food, spend time gently coaxing him to eat something. If he leaves his food, take it away and try it later. Do not leave it down for him all of the time or he may get used to turning his nose up at it. The next time you put some food down for him, he is more likely to be hungry.

The puppy is following you as you have taken the place of his mother. Encourage him to follow you by patting your leg and calling him and when he does, praise him for doing so – but remember to start leaving him for a few minutes after a few days.

 If your puppy is crying, it is probably for one of the following reasons:

* he's hungry or lonely
* he wants attention from you
* he needs to go to the toilet

If it is none of these, then check his body to make sure she hasn't picked up an injury. Labradoodles have a strong instinct to want to bond with humans. That emotional attachment between you and your Labradoodle may grow to become one of the most important aspects of your – and certainly your Labradoodle's - life.

It can be a good idea to let your puppy sleep in your bedroom for the first few nights – but ideally not on the bed.

Dogs are very hierarchical and a Labradoodle puppy needs to learn his place in the household – and it has to be below you in the pecking order if you don't want him to rule your life. Either put him in a crate with a soft blanket or in a high-sided cardboard box he can't climb out of. Put newspapers underneath, as he will not be able to last the night without urinating.

Try not to fuss too much (easier said than done!) If he whimpers, just reassure him with a quiet word. If he cries loudly and tries to get out, he probably needs to go to the toilet. Get up (sorry, this is best) and take him outside. Praise him if he goes to the toilet and take him back inside until you are ready to get up.

After a few nights he should have settled in to his new home, so can be moved to a comfortable place elsewhere in the house. You may have to block your ears for a few nights, as he may whine or call for attention. If you ignore him he will soon get used to sleeping on his own.

The strongest bonding period for a puppy is between eight and 12 weeks of age. The most important factors in bonding with your puppy are TIME spent with him and PATIENCE, even when he makes a mess in the house or chews your furniture.

Remember, he is just a baby and it takes time to learn not to do these things. Spend the time to love and train your Labradoodle pup and you will have a loyal friend for life who will always be there for you and never let you down.

Where Should He Sleep?
If you do decide that your Labradoodle can sleep in your bedroom, put him in a dog bed or crate in a corner of the bedroom. Some owners do allow their dogs to sleep on the bed, but it is neither hygienic nor conducive to a good night's sleep – especially if you have a Standard Labradoodle who will take up most of the bed. It may also create problems with separation anxiety later on. Bite the bullet and make his bed in a separate one to you.

Crate Training a Puppy

If you are unfamiliar with them, crates may seem like a cruel punishment for a dog. On the other hand some people, including some trainers, breeders and people who show dogs, recommend their use to train a puppy and make him feel secure. It's fair to say they are used more in the USA than elsewhere.

If you use a crate, then remember that it is NOT a prison to restrain the dog.

It should only be used in a humane manner and time should be spent to make the puppy feel like the crate is his own safe little haven. If the door is closed on the crate, your Labradoodle must ALWAYS have access to water while inside his crate. He also needs bedding in there and it's a good idea to put a chew in as well. We tried our Max with a crate when he was a young puppy and he emitted ear-piercing howls every time he went in, as if someone was sawing his leg off. In the end, we couldn't bear to hear the noise and so we abandoned the crate.

It is now in the porch at our house and makes a very useful storage place for Wellington boots and running shoes! Now, nine years on, having heard from so many of our American readers about how much their dogs love their crates, I think perhaps we gave up too easily.

If used correctly and if time is spent getting the puppy used to the crate, it can be a valuable tool. But crates are not for every Labradoodle and they should NEVER be used as a means of imprisoning the dog while you are out of the house all day. It would be kinder to have a goldfish than to cage a Labradoodle for most of its life. Doodles are not like hamsters or pet mice which can adapt to life in a cage. These dogs thrive on interaction and being in a cage all day is a miserable existence.

If you do decide to use a crate, maybe to put your dog in for short periods while you leave the house, or at night, the best place to locate it is in the corner of a room, away from cold draughts or too much heat. A Labradoodle likes to be near their pack - which is you. Leave him where he can hear you. Some owners make the crate their dog's only bed, so he feels comfortable and safe in there.

The crate should be large enough to allow your dog to stretch out flat on his side without being cramped, be able to turn round easily and to sit up without hitting his head on the top. If you are buying one that is big enough for your fully-grown Labradoodle, block off part of it while he is small so he feels safe and secure. You can also buy adjustable crate dividers.

Crates aren't for every owner or dog. But, used correctly, a crate can help to:

- Housetrain your dog
- Keep your dog safe when travelling
- Create a doggie bedroom or place where your Labradoodle feels safe.

Here is one method of getting your puppy to accept a crate and then to want to spend time in there. He might not be very happy about going in at first, but he will be a lot easier to crate train than an adult dog, which may have got used to having the run of the house.

- Drop a few tasty puppy treats around and then inside the crate.
- Put your puppy's favourite bedding in there.
- Keep the door open.
- Give all of your puppy's meals to him inside the crate. Keep the door open.
- Place a chew or treat INSIDE the crate and close the door while your pup is OUTSIDE the crate. He'll be desperate to get in, so open the door, let him in and praises him. Fasten a long-lasting chew inside the crate and leave the door open. Let your puppy go inside and spend some time eating the chew.
- After a while, close the crate door and feed him some treats through the mesh while he is in there. At first just do it for a few seconds at a time, then gradually increase the time. If you do it too fast, he will become distressed.
- Slowly build up the amount of time he is in the crate. For the first few days, stay in the room, then gradually leave the room for a short time, first one minute, then three, then 10, 30 minutes and so on.

Next Steps

* Put your dog in his crate at regular intervals during the day - up to a maximum of two hours.

* Don't crate only when you are leaving the house. Place the dog in the crate while you are home as well. Use it as a 'safe zone'. By using the crate both when you are home and while you are

gone, your dog becomes comfortable in the crate and not worried that you won't come back, or that you are leaving him alone. This also helps to prevent separation anxiety later.

* Give him a chew and remove his collar, tags and anything else which could become caught in an opening or between the bars.

* Make it clear to any children that the crate is NOT a playhouse for them, but a 'special room' for the dog,

* Although the crate is your dog's haven and safe place, it must not be off-limits to humans. You should be able to reach inside at any time.

The next points are important if crate training is to succeed:

* Do not let the dog immediately out of the crate while he is barking or he will think that barking is the key to opening the door to the crate.
* Wait until the barking or whining has stopped for at least 10 seconds before letting him out.

If you do decide to use a crate, remember that a dog is not normally a caged animal. Use the crate for limited periods and only if your dog is comfortable in there. NEVER force a dog to go in and then lock him in for hours on end. Better to find him a new, happier home.

Following these guidelines is a good start – but it is only the beginning. Read the other chapters on how to care for and train your puppy so that you and your new best friend can enjoy many years of happiness together.

4. Labradoodles for Allergy Sufferers

Hypoallergenic

You've got or are thinking about getting a Labradoodle. They look cute, they make excellent family pets and you've heard they are non-shedding and 'hypoallergenic', meaning allergy sufferers don't have a reaction to them.

Unfortunately, this last statement is largely untrue for a number of reasons. Let's look at the topic more closely. Firstly, the official definition of the word **hypoallergenic** is *"having a decreased tendency to provoke an allergic reaction"*. In other words there is **no cast iron guarantee** that an allergy or asthma sufferer won't suffer a reaction to a particular dog or type of dog.

It is true that if you choose a hypoallergenic breed, you are less likely to have an allergic reaction. But allergies vary from person to person and coats vary from dog to dog. This is particularly true with the Labradoodle, which is not a breed, but a crossbreed, where there are even more variables.

There are three main coat types with Labradoodles – hair, wool and fleece - and then there are further variations within these three types. For example, a hair coat can be straight, wiry or wavy and a fleece coat can be almost straight, wavy or curly.

It is difficult to predict what sort of coat your Labradoodle pup will grow up to have. The type of coat may vary even within pups of the same litter and often a puppy's coat will change before he reaches adulthood. While a Poodle is regarded as a hypoallergenic breed, a Labrador is not. If your pup takes after his Labrador parents or grandparents, he will most likely moult.

There is also a difference between a first cross (F1) and a multigeneration (multigen) cross. An F1 cross has a good chance of having a coat with at least some similarities to that of the Labrador parent. Australian Labradoodle breeders and other breeders of multigen pups may claim they are allergy friendly and don't moult. While this may be true for some dogs, it is certainly not true of all Australian Labradoodles. According to the Kennel Clubs of both the USA and UK, there is no such thing as a non-shedding dog.

No breeder can guarantee that a specific Labradoodle will be suitable for an individual who suffers from dog allergies. However, it is true to say that when **responsible** breeders of multigen Labradoodles select their breeding stock, coat is an important factor.

There is plenty anecdotal evidence that many of these dogs shed little or no hair and do not trigger a reaction with many allergy sufferers. But each individual case is different.

Allergies are on the increase. Amazingly, 50 million Americans are allergy sufferers, according to the Asthma and Allergy Foundation of America.

One in five of these (10 million people) are pet allergy sufferers. In the UK, pets are the second most important cause of allergy in the home, with 40% of asthmatic children reacting to dogs.

Most people think that people are allergic to animal hair, but that's not true. What they are actually allergic to are proteins - or allergens. These are secreted by the animal's oil glands and then shed with the dander, which is actually dead skin cells. They are also found in dog saliva and urine, and if you are allergic to either, you are unlikely ever to be able to successfully share your home with a dog. But the good news for dog lovers is that more people are allergic to cats!

The Facts
It is possible for pet allergy sufferers to enjoy living with a dog without spending all of their time sneezing, wheezing, itching or breaking out in rashes. Millions of people are proving the case.

Some types of dogs are definitely better for allergy sufferers. Any dog can cause an allergic reaction, although a low-shedding, hypoallergenic purebred such as a Poodle is a much better choice than a breed which moults. A Labradoodle may take after a Poodle and shed only a little or may shed a great deal, like a Labrador.

You may be fine with a Labradoodle puppy, as tiny puppies don't shed. But often the coat changes in adulthood and this could trigger a severe allergic reaction later on. It would indeed cause distress if you were suddenly allergic to your adult Labradoodle, who has become a dearly-loved member of your family. If you have any doubts at all about a puppy - even a tiny reaction - don't get him.

We strongly advise against selecting a Labradoodle solely because you believe the dog will not trigger your allergies. There are no guarantees. For those people with consistent or severe allergies, another option would be to consider a pure bred hypoallergenic breed and then follow certain steps to select a breeder and puppy.

Choosing a suitable dog is not completely straightforward and you do have to put in extra time to make sure that you pick the right dog and maybe make a few adjustments to your home as well.

No dog is totally non-shedding
No dog is totally hypoallergenic

Two further points to consider are that people's pet allergies vary greatly. Pet allergy sufferers may react differently to different breeds **as well as individual dogs within that breed.** A sufferer may be fine with one puppy yet have a reaction to another in the same litter; this is especially true of Labradoodles where the pups may have different coats.

All dogs - even so-called 'hairless' dogs - have hair, dander (dead skin cells, like dandruff), saliva and urine. Therefore all dogs *can* cause allergic reactions. But not all dogs do. Some hypoallergenic dog breeds do not affect pet allergy sufferers as much because of the type or amount of hair that they shed. Hypoallergenic dogs virtually do not moult. (You might find the *occasional* dog hair or small fur ball around the house).

Choosing a puppy

Find a reputable breeder and first of all ask if you could visit their adult dogs. Make sure there are no cats around which could also trigger allergies. If you are determined to stick with Labradoodles, spend time with both parents of any pup that you are considering buying, and also try to spend time with the different coat types to see which, if any, cause a reaction.

Choose an experienced breeder that will have a better knowledge of how puppy coats will develop as the dog grows up. Then spend some time alone with the specific pup you are thinking of getting to determine if you have a reaction, which may be up to two days later.

Handle the dog, rub your hands on your face, and lick your hands after you have handled the dog in order to absorb as much potential allergen as you can on your short visit.

Go back and visit the breeder's at least once or twice more before you make that life-changing commitment to buy the puppy. Take an old towel or piece of cloth and rub the puppy with it, Take this home with you and handle it to see if you get a delayed reaction.

Check with the breeder to see if you can return the pup within a certain time period were you to have a reaction to him back at home. You cannot expect the breeder to take the dog back if the allergies only occur once he has reached adulthood.

Everyone with pet allergies can tolerate a certain amount of allergens (things they are allergic to). If that person is just below his or her tolerance, any additional allergen will push him over the edge, triggering a reaction.
So if you reduce the general allergen load in the home, you'll be much more successful when you bring your dog home.

Top 10 Tips for Reducing Pet Allergens

1. Get a HEPA air cleaner in the bedroom and/or main living room. HEPA stands for High Efficiency Particle Air - a type of air filter that removes 99.97% of all particles.

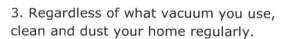

2. Use a HEPA vacuum cleaner. Neither the HEPA air nor vacuum cleaner is cheap, but if you suffer allergies and really want to share your life and home with a dog, they are worth considering. Both will dramatically improve the quality of the air you breathe in your home.

3. Regardless of what vacuum you use, clean and dust your home regularly.

4. Keep the dog out of your bedroom. We spend around a third of our lives here and keeping animals out can greatly reduce allergic reactions.

5. Do not allow your dog on the couch, bed or any other furniture. Keep him out of the car, or if this is not possible, use car seat covers or a blanket on the seat.

6. Brush your pet regularly - always outdoors -and regularly clean his bedding. Avoid using normal washing powder, as it may trigger a reaction in dogs with sensitive skin.

7. Keep your dog's skin healthy by regularly feeding a good multivitamin and a fatty acid supplement, such as fish oil.

8. Consider using an allergy-reducing spray such as Allerpet, which helps to cleanse the dog's fur hair of dander, saliva and sebaceous gland secretions. There are also products to reduce allergens from carpets, curtains and furniture.

9. Avoid contact with other dogs and always wash your hands after you have handled any dog, including your own.

10. Consult your doctor and discuss possible immunotherapy or medication. There are medical advanced being made in the treatment of allergies and a range of tables, sprays and even injections are currently available.

Experts aren't sure whether bathing your dog has any effect on allergy symptoms. Some studies have shown that baths reduce the amount of airborne dander, while others haven't found a difference.

You can certainly try weekly baths and see what happens; just make sure that it's not the person with dog allergies doing the bathing.

Of course, the only sure-fire way to GUARANTEE no allergic reaction is not to have a dog.

If you have allergies and are determined to go ahead and share your home with Man's Best Friend, then the safest route is to select a non-shedding breed. Actually, there is no such thing as totally non-shedding either.

But the American Kennel Club (AKC) and Kennel Club UK both publish lists of **"breeds that generally do well with people with allergies."**

Many new types of crossbreed dogs are springing up, most of them bred with a Poodle, and some breeders are making claims about them being non-shedding. But as you now know, there is no such thing – even with a purebred (pedigree) dog.

We risk the wrath of Doodle lovers by mentioning other types of dog. We are not recommending one over another, simply supplying you with the information to make an informed decision.

Schnoodles
If you definitely don't want a purebred dog, then you might want to consider a crossbreed with hypoallergenic parents on both sides, and that's the Schnoodle, a cross between a Schnauzer and a Poodle. But be warned, there's no guarantee with a Schnoodle either.

There are some similarities in appearance and sizes between Labradoodles and Schnoodles. It's hard to say what a typical one looks like as they range in size from very small to very large and their coats come in a variety of colours, just like Labradoodles.

Schnoodle

There are three types of Poodle – Standard, Miniature and Toy and three types of Schnauzer - Giant, Standard and Miniature. A Schnoodle can be any combination of these. The results are four types of Schnoodle: **Giant, Standard, Miniature** or **Toy**. The most common of these used to be the Miniature, however Giant Schnoodles are becoming increasingly popular.

A Giant Schnoodle is a cross between a Standard Poodle and a Giant Schnauzer. A fully grown one will weigh as much as 65-80lbs and stand 24 to 27 inches high at the shoulders.

A Toy Schnoodle is a cross between a Toy Poodle and a small Miniature Schnauzer. It is 10 inches or under at the shoulders weighs less than 10 pounds.

The many faces of the Schnoodle

Some breeders think the Poodle takes the chunkiness out of the Schnauzer, while the Schnauzer takes the pointed head away from the Poodle. Although the Schnoodle is a crossbreed and there are no written breed characteristics, dogs should be well-proportioned and athletic with a keen, bold and lively expression.

The Schnoodle coat comes in many colours: black, white, grey, apricot, chocolate, black with white markings, wheaten, sable, parti (white with patches of colour) or phantom (black and tan like the Doberman). Although there are a variety of colours, the Schnoodle coat is almost always curly or wavy at the very least and generally is minimal shedding.

The Schnoodle temperament will vary from one dog to the next. However, there are some general characteristics that are common with

71

many, if not most. Generally, Schnoodles are happy and playful by nature. Provided they get enough exercise, they are sociable, fun dogs and are becoming increasingly popular as they are usually hypoallergenic and make good companions for humans.

The Schnoodle is an intelligent crossbreed which often has high energy levels and loves playtime. They usually interact well with other dogs and are not normally aggressive by nature. However, as with all puppies, early socialisation with other dogs as well as a wide range of people is important. This teaches your dog to trust and be trusted.

 The Schnoodle temperament mixes the intellect of the Poodle with the companionship and devotion of the Schnauzer. If treated well when young, Schnoodles make loving, loyal and amusing companions. Being eager to please, they are relatively easy to train. Training should be done in short bursts and efforts should be made to keep it interesting, as it may not be easy to keep their concentration for long periods.

They love playing and distractions. Smaller Schnoodles may be happy as lapdogs, whereas the larger ones are friskier and will require more of your time and attention.

Like Schnauzers, Schnoodles like being with people and involved at the centre of family life. They are not happy when left alone for long periods. If you are out at work all day, a Schnoodle may not be a suitable choice – and neither will a Labradoodle as they also love being with people.

Like the Labradoodle, the Schnoodle is a crossbreed or hybrid. Puppies are not eligible for registration with purebred or pedigree registries such as the American, Canadian or UK Kennel Clubs. However, in the USA they can be registered with the American Canine Hybrid Club.

List of Hypoallergenic Dogs

While the UK and American Kennel Clubs do not guarantee that a person will NOT have an allergic reaction to a particular dog, certain hypoallergenic and non-shedding dog breeds are generally thought to be better for allergy sufferers.

In terms of purebreds, the Kennel Clubs do not make any claims about hypoallergenic dogs or breeds. But they both publish lists.

Here are the lists, they are all purebred dogs.

American Kennel Club List
The American Kennel Club's list of "breeds that generally do well with people with allergies" is:

Bedlington Terrier

Bichon Frise

Chinese Crested

Irish Water Spaniel

Kerry Blue Terrier

Maltese

Poodle (Toy, Miniature and Standard)

Portuguese Water Dog

Schnauzer (Giant, Standard and Miniature)

Soft Coated Wheaten Terrier

Xoloitzcuintli (FSS Breed)

Portuguese Water Dog

Kennel Club (UK) List
The KC has this to say: ***"For those owners who wish to obtain a dog which SUPPOSEDLY does not shed its coat, one of these listed breeds may be a suitable choice:"***

Gundog Group
Lagotto Romagnolo

Irish Water Spaniel

Spanish Water Dog (Like President Obama's Bo, sometimes referred to as 'the Labradoodle look-alike')

Working Group
Bouvier des Flandres

Giant Schnauzer

Yorkshire Terrier

Portuguese Water Dog

Russian Black Terrier

Pastoral Group
Hungarian Puli

Komondor

Toy Group
Bichon Frise

Bolognese

Chinese Crested

Coton de Tulear

Havanese

Maltese

Yorkshire Terrier

Utility Group

Lhasa Apso

Intermediate Mexican Hairless

Miniature Mexican Hairless

Standard Mexican Hairless

Miniature Schnauzer

Standard Poodle

Toy Poodle

Miniature Poodle

Shih Tzu Tibetan Terrier

Terrier Group
Bedlington Terrier

Dandie Dinmont Terrier

Lhasa Apso

Mexican Hairless

Bedlington Terrier

Glen of Imaal Terrier

Sealyham Terrier

Soft Coated Wheaten Terrier

Whatever type of dog you decide to get, spend some time with the individual beforehand to see if you have any reaction and visit more than once. Let the puppy lick your face or touch your face with your hands after handling the pup.

Wheaten Terriers

Wait a couple of days after each contact session. If there's still no reaction, you might be one of the numerous allergy sufferers who is lucky enough to share their home with Man's Best Friend.

Remember:

* No breed or crossbreed is totally non-shedding

* No breed or crossbreed is totally hypoallergenic

---

5. Feeding Your Labradoodle

Choices

The whole topic of feeding your dog the right diet is something of a minefield. Owners are bombarded with endless choices as well as countless adverts from dog food companies, who all claim that theirs is best.

The simple answer is that no one food is best for all dogs. But the question is: Which food is best for your dog?

There are many different options. The most popular manufactured foods include dry complete diets, tinned food, with or without a biscuit mixer, and semi-moist.

Some dog foods contain only natural ingredients. Then there is the option of feeding your dog a home-made diet; some owners swear by a raw diet, while others feed their dogs vegetarian food.

Within the manufactured options, there are many different qualities of food. Usually you get what you pay for, so a more expensive food is more likely to provide better nutrition for your dog - in terms of minerals, nutrients and high quality meats - than a cheap one, which will most likely contain a lot of grain.

Dried foods (also called kibble in the USA) tend to be less expensive than other foods. They have improved a lot over the last few years and some of the more expensive ones are now a good choice for a healthy, complete diet. Dried foods also contain the least fat and the most preservatives.

Our dog Max, who has inhalant allergies, is on a quality dried food called James Wellbeloved. It contains natural ingredients and the manufacturers claim it is hypoallergenic, so good for dogs with allergies. Max seems to do well on it, but not all dogs thrive on dried food. We tried several other foods first, it is a question of each owner finding the best food for their dog.

TIP: Beware of buying a food just because it is described as '*premium*', many manufacturers blithely use this word, but there are no official guidelines as to what premium means. Always check the ingredients on any food sack, packet or tin to see which ingredients are listed first, and it should be meat or poultry, not grain.

If you are in the USA, look for a dog food which has been endorsed by AAFCO (Association of American Feed Control Officials).

In general, tinned foods are 60-70% water. Often semi-moist foods contain a lot of sugar and artificial substances, which is maybe why some dogs seem to love them!

Choosing the right food for your Labradoodle is important, it will influence his health, coat and even temperament. There are also three stages of your dog's life to consider when feeding: puppy, adult and senior (also called veteran). Each of these represents a different physical stage of his life and you need to choose the right food to cope with his body during each particular phase.

Also, a pregnant female will require a special diet to cope with the extra demands on her body. This is especially important as she nears the latter stages of pregnancy.

We are not recommending one brand of dog food over another, but we do have some general tips to help you choose what to feed your Labradoodle, before we look at different food types in more detail.

Top 12 Tips for Feeding your Labradoodle

1.Some Labradoodles have sensitive or problem skin or allergies. A cheap dog food, often bulked up with grain, will only make this worse. If this is the case, bite the bullet and choose a high quality – usually more expensive - food. You'll probably save money in vets' bills in the long run and your dog will be happier.

2.Don't pick a food where meat or poultry content is NOT the first item listed on the bag. Foods with lots of cheap cereals or sugar are not the best choice for many dogs, particularly sensitive ones.

3.Frequency of feeds should be based on size. A small dog like a Miniature Labradoodle has a fast metabolism and burns off his food calories quicker than a large dog like the Standard. Generally, adult Miniature and Medium Labradoodles should be fed twice a day, while Standard Labradoodles only need to be fed once a day, although many

Standard owners prefer to give two smaller feeds. Puppies of all sizes need to be fed more often.

4. Establish a feeding regime and stick to it. Dogs like routine. If you are feeding twice a day, feed once in the morning and then again at tea-time. Stick to the same times of day. Do not give the last feed too late, or your dog's body will not have chance to process or burn off the food before sleeping.

He will also need a walk or letting out in the garden after his second feed to allow him to go to the toilet. Feeding at the same times every day also helps your dog establish a toilet regime.

5. Take away the food between meals. Your Labradoodle may become a fussy eater if you leave his food down all day. Imagine if your dinner was left on the table for hours until you finished it. Returning to the table two or three hours later would not be such a tempting prospect, but coming back for a fresh meal would be far more appetising.

Also, when food is left down all day, some dogs seem to take the food for granted and lose their appetite. Then they begin to leave the food and you are at your wits' end trying to find a food that they will actually eat. Put the bowl with the food down twice a day and then take it up after 20 minutes – even if he has left some. If he is healthy and hungry, he will look forward to his next meal and soon stop leaving food. If your dog does not eat anything for days, it could well be a sign that something is wrong with him.

6. Do not feed too many titbits and treats between meals. This is unhealthy for the dog, affects his balanced diet and can lead to obesity. Stick to regular mealtimes. Try to avoid feeding your dog from the table or your plate, as this encourages attention-seeking behaviour such as begging, barking and drooling.

7. NEVER feed the following items to your dog: grapes, raisins, chocolate, onions, Macadamia nuts, any fruits with seeds or stones, tomatoes, avocadoes, rhubarb, tea, coffee or alcohol. ALL of these are poisonous to dogs.

8. If you feed leftovers to your dog, feed them INSTEAD of a balanced meal, not as well as. High quality dog foods are already made up to

provide all the nutrients, vitamins, minerals and calories that your dog needs. Feeding titbits or leftovers may be too rich for your dog in addition to his regular diet and cause him to scratch or have other problems.

9. If you switch to a new food, do the transition over a week or so. Unlike humans, dogs' digestive systems cannot handle sudden changes in diet. Begin by gradually mixing some of the new food in with the old and increase the proportion so that after seven to eight days, all the food is the new one.

10. Check your dog's weight regularly. Obesity in Labradoodles, as well as being generally unhealthy, can lead to the development of some serious

health issues, such as diabetes. Although the weight will vary from one dog to another and from Miniature to Medium to Standard, a good rule of thumb is that your Labradoodle's tummy should be higher than his rib cage. If his belly hangs down below it, he is overweight.

11. Check your dog's faeces (poo!) If his diet is suitable, the food should be easily digested and produce dark brown, firm stools. If your dog produces soft or light stools, or has wind or diarrhoea, then the diet may not suit him, so consult your vet for advice.

12. And finally, always make sure that your Labradoodle has access to clean, fresh water. Change the water regularly.

One note for owners of large Standard Labradoodles – particularly those who rush their food - is that they may wish to consider putting his feeding bowls on a small stand or bench so they are at shoulder height. Large, deep-chested dogs are susceptible to bloat, a serious condition which occurs when they take in too much air while feeding. Ask your vet's opinion on this.

Types of Dog Food

We are what we eat! That's not quite true with dogs and their diet, but it is true that the right food is a very important part of a healthy lifestyle. It can affect health, coat and skin, energy levels and temperament.

There are several different types of food you can feed your Doodle: dry, semi-moist, canned, frozen or freeze-dried are just some of the options. Or you might decide to feed a home-made or raw diet; this is an option increasingly being considered by owners of Labradoodles with food allergies or skin conditions.

Dry dog food

 – often called kibble in the USA – is a popular choice, particularly for large dogs who get through a lot of food. It comes in different flavours and with differing ingredients to suit the various stages of a dog's life, it's also less expensive than many other foods. It's worth paying for a high quality dry food as cheaper ones may contain a lot of cereal. Cheap foods are often false economy, particularly if your Labradoodle does not tolerate grain/cereal very well. It may also mean that you have to feed larger quantities to ensure your dog gets sufficient nutrients.

Canned food

Another popular choice. It's often very popular with dogs too! They love the taste and it generally comes in a variety of flavours. Canned food is often mixed with dry kibble, and a small amount may be added to a dog on a dry food diet if he has lost interest in food.

It tends to be more expensive than dried food and many owners don't like the mess. With smaller dogs, a part-opened tin may have to be kept in the fridge between meals and it can have an overpowering smell when you open the fridge door. As with dry food, read the label closely. Generally, you get what you pay for and the origins of cheap canned dog food may be somewhat dubious.

Semi-Moist

These are commercial dog foods shaped like pork chops, salamis, burgers or other meaty foods and they are the least nutritional of all dog foods. They are full of sugars, artificial flavourings and colourings to help make them visually appealing. While you may give your dog one as an occasional treat, they are not a diet in themselves and do not provide the nutrition that your Labradoodle needs.

Freeze dried

This is often made by frozen food manufacturers for owners who like the convenience of it – it keeps for six months to a year - or for those going on a trip with their dog. It says 'freeze-dried' on the packet and is highly palatable, but the freeze-drying process bumps up the cost.

Home Cooked

Some dog owners want the ability to be in complete control of their dog's diet, know exactly what their dog is eating and to be absolutely sure that his nutritional needs are being met. Feeding your dog a home-cooked diet is time consuming and expensive, and the difficult thing – as with the raw diet - is sticking to it once you have started out with the best of intentions.

But many owners think the extra effort is worth the peace of mind. If you decide to go ahead, you should learn about canine nutrition to ensure your dog gets all his vital nutrients.

Raw Food

If your dog is not doing well on a commercially-prepared dog food, you might consider a raw diet. There is evidence that they are becoming increasingly popular among owners. Raw food diets emulate the way dogs ate before the existence of commercial dog foods. After all, dry, canned and other styles of cooked food for dogs were mainly created as a means of convenience. Unfortunately, this convenience sometimes can affect a dog's health.

However, raw diets are not without controversy. Supporters argue that a carefully planned raw diet gives the dog numerous health benefits, including a healthier coat, more energy, cleaner teeth and a lack of bad breath and doggy odour.

Critics say that that the risks of nutritional imbalance, intestinal problems and food-borne illnesses, caused by handling and feeding raw meat, outweigh any benefits. Scientifically, the jury is still out.

However, some nutritionists do believe that dogs that eat raw whole foods tend to be healthier than those on other diets. They say there are inherent beneficial enzymes, vitamins, minerals and other qualities in meats, fruits, vegetables and grains in their natural forms that are denatured or destroyed when cooked. Many also believe dogs are less likely to have allergic reactions to the ingredients on this diet.

Frozen food can be a valuable aid to the raw diet. The food is highly palatable, made from high quality ingredients and dogs usually love it. The downside is that not all pet food stores stock it and it is expensive.

One type of raw diet is the BARF diet (*Biologically Appropriate Raw Food* or *Bones And Raw Food)*, created by Dr Ian Billinghurst. A typical BARF diet is made up of 60-80% of raw meaty bones (bones with about 50% meat, such as chicken neck, back and wings) and 20-40% of fruit and vegetables, offal, meat, eggs or dairy foods.

If you are interested in exploring a raw food diet for your dog, consult your vet to see if your dog is a suitable candidate and speak to other Labradoodle owners to find out exactly what is involved. There are many discussions on this topic online, including at ***labradoodle-dogs.net/forums***
Only start a raw diet if you are sure you have the time (and money) to keep it going.

Dog Food Allergies

Symptoms
Dog food allergies affect about one in 10 dogs. They are the third most common allergy for our canine companions after flea bite allergies and atophy (inhaled allergies). While there's no strong link between specific breeds and food allergies, there is some anecdotal evidence from owners of an increase in the number of Labradoodles with food allergies or intolerances.

In 2013, the UK Labradoodle Association canvassed opinion online on the subject of food allergies and sensitivities. They asked owners to agree or disagree with statements which included:

- My Doodle is sensitive/allergic to some foods
- My Doodle gets skin/ear/stomach

problems with some food
- My Doodle can't tolerate wheat/corn/grain
- My Doodle is cream/apricot.

The owners' responses can be read here:
www.labradoodle.org.uk/forum/viewtopic.php?t=26011

Food allergies affect males and females in equal measure, as well as neutered and intact animals. They can show up when your dog is five months or 12 years old - although the vast majority start when the dog is between two and six years old. It is not uncommon for dogs with food allergies to also have other types of allergies.

If your dog is not well, how do you know if the problem lies with his food or not? Here are some common symptoms of food allergies:

- Itchy skin (this is the most common)
- Excessive scratching
- Ear infections
- Hair loss
- Hot patches of skin
- Recurring skin infections
- Increased bowel movements (maybe twice as often as usual)

Allergies or Intolerance?
There's a difference between dog food *allergies* and dog food *intolerance*:

Typical reactions to allergies are skin problems and/or itching
Typical reactions to intolerance are diarrhoea and/or vomiting

Dog food intolerance can be compared to people who get diarrhoea or an upset stomach from eating spicy food. Both can be cured by a change to a diet specifically suited to your dog, although a food allergy may be harder to get to the root cause of. As they say in the canine world: "One dog's meat is another dog's poison".

Causes
Certain ingredients are more likely to cause allergies than others. In order of the most common triggers for dogs they are:

Beef
Dairy products
Chicken
Wheat
Eggs
Corn
Soy

Unfortunately, these most common offenders are also the most common ingredients in dog foods! By the way, don't think if you put your dog on a rice and lamb dog food diet that it will automatically cure the problem. It might, but then again there's a fair chance it won't. The reason lamb and rice were thought to be less likely to cause allergies is simply because they have not traditionally been included in dog food recipes - therefore less dogs had reactions to them.

Diagnosis

As you can see from the symptoms listed above, the diagnosis for food allergies is fairly straightforward. The problem is that these conditions may also be symptoms of other problems such as atophy (breathed-in allergies), flea bite allergies, intestinal problems, mange and yeast or bacterial infections.

You can have a blood test on your dog, but many vets now believe that this is not accurate enough.

If you can rule out all of the above, and you have tried switching diet without much success, then a food trial can be started. This is usually the option of last resort, due to the amount of time and attention that it requires. It is also called '***an exclusion diet'*** and is the only truly accurate way of finding out if your dog has a food allergy and what is causing it.

Before you do this, try a hypoallergenic dog food, either commercial or home-made. There are a number of these on the market and they all have the word '*hypoallergenic* ' in the name.

Although usually more expensive, hypoallergenic dog food ingredients do not include common allergens such as wheat protein or soya, thereby minimising the risk of an allergic reaction.

Food Trials

It is important that you keep a diary during a food trial to record any changes in your Labradoodle's symptoms, behaviour or habits. A food trial involves feeding one specific food for at least 12 weeks, something the dog has never eaten before, such as rabbit and rice or venison and potato. The food should contain no added colouring, preservatives or flavourings.

There are a number of these commercial diets on the market as well as specialised diets that have proteins and carbohydrates broken down into such small molecular sizes that they no longer trigger an allergic reaction. These are called *'limited antigen'* or *'hydrolysed protein'* diets.

Home-made diets are another option as you can strictly control the ingredients. The difficult thing is that this must be the **only thing** the dog eats during the trial.
Any treats or snacks make the whole thing is a waste of time. During the trial, you shouldn't allow your dog to roam freely, as you cannot control what he is eating or drinking when he is out of sight outdoors.

Food Trial Tips
Only the recommended diet must be fed. Do NOT give:

- Treats
- Rawhides
- Pigs' ears
- Cows' hooves
- Flavoured medications (including heartworm treatments) or supplements
- Flavoured toothpastes
- Flavoured plastic toys

If you want to give a treat, use the recommended diet. (Tinned diets can be frozen in chunks or baked and then used as treats.). If you have other dogs, either feed them all on the food trial diet or feed other dogs in an entirely different location.

If you have a cat, don't let the dog near the cat litter tray. Keep your pet out of the room when you are eating. Even small amounts of food dropped on the floor or licked off of a plate can ruin an elimination trial, meaning you'll have to start all over again.

How Much Food?
This is another question which we are often asked on our website. The answer is... there is no easy answer! The correct amount of food for your dog depends on a number of factors:

- Breed
- Gender
- Age
- Energy levels
- Amount of daily exercise
- Health

- Environment
- Number of dogs in house
- Quality of the food

Some breeds have a higher metabolic rate than others. Labradoodles are generally regarded as dogs with a moderate activity level, but this is a bit misleading, as energy levels vary tremendously from individual dog to dog.

Generally smaller dogs have faster metabolisms so require a higher amount of food per pound of body weight. Female dogs are slightly more prone to putting on weight than male dogs.

Some people say that dogs which have been spayed or neutered are more likely to put on weight, although this is disputed by others. Growing puppies and young dogs need more food than senior dogs with a slower lifestyle.

Every dog is different, you can have two Labradoodles and one may be very energetic while the other has a more placid temperament. The

energetic dog will burn off more calories. Maintaining a healthy body weight for dogs – and humans – is all about balancing what you take in with what you burn off.

If your Labradoodle is exercised three times a day and allowed to run and play off the lead with other dogs, he will need more calories than a Labradoodle which gets one walk on the lead every day.

Certain health conditions such as an underactive thyroid, diabetes, arthritis or heart disease can lead to dogs putting on weight, so their food has to be adjusted accordingly.

Just like us, a dog kept in a very cold environment will need more calories to keep warm than a dog in a warm climate. They burn extra calories in keeping themselves warm.

Here's an interesting fact: a dog kept on his own is more likely to be overweight than a dog kept with other dogs, as he receives all of the food-based attention.

Cheaper foods usually recommend feeding more to your dog, as much of the food is made up of cereals, which are not doing much except bulking up the weight of the food – and possibly triggering allergies in your Labradoodle.

Because there are so many factors involved, there is no simple answer to how much to feed. However, below we have listed a broad guideline of the average amount of **calories** a Labradoodle with medium energy and activity levels needs.

Thanks to *'Better Food for Dogs - A Complete Cookbook and Nutrition Guide'* by D Bastin et al, published by Robert Rose, Inc for the following information and daily feeding guide:

"The standard weight of each breed is stated in brackets. If your dog falls beyond the standard weight due to under or overfeeding, take the opportunity of diet change as part of your dog's weight management program.

Target your dog at the highest acceptable weight of his breed class to begin with if he or she is overweight. On the other hand, if your dog is underweight, target your dog at the lowest weight acceptable weight of his breed class to begin with.

Adjust the energy level gradually toward the middle of the range.

Note: if your dog's weight problems are caused by certain health problems, pregnancy or other conditions, consult your vet before implementing any weight management program as this must be supervised by your vet."

Disclaimer: This chart is designed to give a broad guideline as to the amount of food to feed a dog every day based on size. As the Labradoodle is a crossbreed, there are more variations than within registered pure breeds. Check your dog's ideal weight before embarking on a feeding regime. Consult your vet if your dog loses or gains considerable weight.

Canine Calorie Counter

BREED	WEIGHT	ENERGY
Miniature	15 lb / 6.8 Kg	463 - 556 Kcal
Labradoodle	20 lb / 9.0 Kg	575 - 690 Kcal
7 – 13 kg	25 lbs / 11.3 Kg	680 - 816 Kcal
	30 lbs / 13.6 Kg	779 - 935 Kcal
Medium	30 lbs / 13.6 Kg	779 - 935 Kcal
Labradoodle	35 lbs / 15.8 Kg	875 - 1050 Kcal
13– 20 kg	40 lbs / 18.1 Kg	965 - 1158 Kcal
	45 lbs / 20.4 Kg	1056 - 1267 Kcal
Standard	50 lbs / 22.6 Kg	1143 - 1327 Kcal
Labradoodle	55 lbs / 24.9 Kg	1228 - 1437 Kcal
23 – 30 kg	60 lbs / 27.2 Kg	1310 - 1537 Kcal
(50 – 65lbs)	65 lbs / 29.5 Kg	1392 - 1670 Kcal
Bigger	70 lbs / 31.7 Kg	1471 - 1766 Kcal
Labradoodles	75 lbs / 34.0 Kg	1549 - 1859 Kcal
30 – 38 kg	80 lbs / 36.27 Kg	1626 - 1951 Kcal
(65 – 85lbs)	85 lbs / 38.6 Kg	1701 - 2042 Kcal

We feed our dog a dried hypoallergenic dog food made by James Wellbeloved in England. Max has seasonal allergies which make him scratch, but he seems to do pretty well on this food. Here are James Wellbeloved's recommended feeding amounts for dogs, listed in kilograms and grams.

28.3 grams = 1 ounce. 1kg = 2.2 pounds

The number on the left is the dog's **adult weight** in kilograms. So an adult Standard Labradoodle would probably be somewhere between 23kg (50lbs) and 30kg (65lbs), depending on how big the parents were and whether the dog is a male or female.

The numbers on the right are the amount of daily food in grams that an average dog with average energy levels requires, measured in grams (divide this by 28.3 to get the amount in ounces). For example, a 3-month-old Standard Labradoodle puppy which will grow into a 30kg adult would require around 400 grams of food per day (14 ounces).

NOTE: These are only very general guidelines, your dog may need more or less than this.

 For example, we feed our dog more than the recommended amount, as he is active and exercised three times a day. If he started gaining weight we would reduce the amount. Use the chart as a guideline only and if your dog appears to lose or gain weight, adjust his or her feeds accordingly.

Canine Feeding Chart

Puppy

Size	expected adult body weight	Age of Puppy and daily Serving (grams)					
		2 mths	3 mths	4 mths	5 mths	6 mths	> 6 mths
Toy	2kg	50	60	60	60	60	change to adult
Small	5kg	95	115	120	115	115	
Medium	10kg	155	190	195	190	190	change to junior

Size	expected adult body weight	Age of Puppy and daily Serving (grams)					
		2 mths	3 mths	4 mths	5 mths	6 mths	> 6 mths
Medium/Large	20kg	240	305	325	320	315	change to junior /large breed jnr
Large	30kg	300	400	435	435	430	
Large/Giant	40kg	345	480	530	540	530	change to large breed junior
	50kg	390	550	615	630	630*	
Giant	60kg	430	610	690	720*	720*	
	70kg	460	675	765*	800*	810*	

Junior

Size	expected adult body weight (kg)	Age of Puppy and daily Serving (g)						
		6 mths	7 mths	8 mths	10 mths	12 mths	14 mths	16 mths
Medium	10	200	195	185	175	change to adult		
Medium/Large*	20	330	325	310	290	300	change to adult/large breed adult	
	30	455	440	430	400	400		
Large*	40	565	555	540	520	485	495	change to large breed adult

Adult

Size	Body Weight (kg)	Daily Serving (g)
Toy	2-5	55-115
Small	5-10	115-190
Medium	10-20	190-320
Medium/Large	20-30	320-430
Large*	30*-40*	430*-520*
Large/Giant*	40*-50*	520*-620*
	50*-60*	620*-710*
Giant*	60*-70*	710*-790*
	70*-90*	790*-950*

Overweight Dogs

Overweight dogs are sadly susceptible to a range of illnesses. According to James Howie, Veterinary Advisor to Lintbells, some of the main ones are:

Joint disease – excessive body weight may increase joint stress which is a risk factor in joint degeneration (arthrosis), as is cruciate disease (knee ligament rupture). Joint disease tends to lead to a reduction in exercise which then increases the likelihood of weight gain which reduces exercise further. A vicious cycle is created.

 Overfeeding large breed dogs, such as Standard Labradoodles, while they are growing can lead to various problems, including worsening of hip dysplasia. Weight management may be the only measure required to control clinical signs in some cases.

Heart and lung problems – fatty deposits within the chest cavity and excessive circulating fat play important roles in the development of cardio-respiratory and cardiovascular disease.

Diabetes – resistance to insulin has been shown to occur in overweight dogs, leading to a greater risk of diabetes mellitus.

Tumours – obesity increases the risk of mammary tumours in female dogs.

Liver disease – fat degeneration may result in liver insufficiency.

Reduced Lifespan - one of the most serious proven findings in obesity studies is that obesity in both humans and dogs reduces lifespan.

Exercise intolerance – this is also a common finding with overweight dogs, which can compound an obesity problem as less calories are burned and are therefore stored, leading to further weight gain.

Most Labradoodles are very attached to their humans. However, beware of going too far in regarding your dog a member of the family. It has been shown that dogs that are perceived to be 'family members' (i.e. anthropomorphosis) by the owner are at greater risk of becoming overweight. This is because attention given to the dog often results in food being given as well.

The important thing to remember is that many of the problems associated with being overweight are reversible. Increasing exercise increases the calories burned, which in turn reduces weight. If you do put your dog on a diet, the reduced amount of food will also mean reduced nutrients, so he may need a supplement during this time.

Feeding Puppies

Puppy foods
Feeding your Labradoodle puppy the right diet is important to help his young body and bones grow strong and healthy. Puppyhood is a time of rapid growth and development and puppies require different levels of nutrients to adult dogs.

For the first six weeks, puppies need milk about five to seven times a day, which they take from their mother. Generally they make some sound if they want to feed. The frequency is reduced when the pup reaches six to eight weeks old.

Puppies should stay with their mothers until seven or eight weeks old before leaving the litter. For the first few days after that, it's a good idea to continue feeding the same puppy food and at the same times as the breeder. Dogs do not adapt to changes in their diet or feeding habits as easily as humans.

You can then slowly change his food based on information from the breeder and your vet. This should be done very gradually by mixing in a little more of the new food each day over a period of seven or eight days. If at any time your puppy starts being sick, has loose stools or is constipated, slow the rate at which you are switching him over. If he continues vomiting, seek veterinary advice as he may have a problem with the food you have chosen.

Because of their special nutritional needs, you should only give your puppy a food   that is approved either just for puppies or for all life stages. If a feed is recommended for adult dogs only, it won't have enough protein and the balance of calcium and other nutrients will not be right for a pup.

Puppy food is very high in calories and nutritional supplements so you want to switch to adult food once he begins to approach maturity. Feeding puppy food too long can result in obesity and orthopaedic problems. There is no set age when the switch should be made. In general, the smaller the dog the faster they reach maturity. Small breeds up to 30 pounds mature at around 10 to 12 months old. Dogs up to 80 pounds, such as large Labradoodles, will reach maturity between 12 to 16 months, although it could be even longer with big-boned Standards – check with your vet on the right time to switch.

Large puppies
Overfeeding large breed dogs, or feeding too many carbohydrates, promotes too-rapid growth which puts stress on joints and can lead to problems such as hip dysplasia. The average Golden Retriever, for example, grows from 14 oz to over 65 lbs within one year – a 70-fold

increase! Human beings take 18 years to do the same thing. If you have a Standard puppy, keep him lean while he is growing.

Most pet nutritionists recommend that big, fast growing puppies eat diets containing at least 30% protein and 9% fat (dry matter basis). The calcium content should be around 1.5% (or 3 grams per1,000 kcal), check the labelling or ask your vet to recommend a feed - but be prepared, he or she may recommend an expensive option available only through them.

For all puppies, but especially large breed ones, remember that treats add calories to the overall diet. Make sure the treats are small and do not contain added calcium – get used to giving fruit and vegetables as treats, these are a healthier option.

Many manufacturers offer a special formula for puppies and sometimes for large breed puppies. You should not overfeed any Labradoodle puppy, but with big Standards the protein, calcium and phosphorus levels may be more critical. It's worth spending time to choose the right fuel to power his healthy development. Think of it as a foundation stone towards future health.

How often?
Establishing a regular feeding routine with your puppy is a good idea, as this will also help to toilet train him. Get him used to regular mealtimes and then let him outside to do his business. Puppies have fast metabolisms, so the results may be pretty quick!

Don't leave food out for the puppy so that he can eat it whenever he wants. You need to be there for the feeds because you want him and his body on a set schedule. Smaller meals are easier for him to digest for and energy levels don't peak and fall so much with frequent feeds.

Puppies under six months of age should be fed three, possible four, times a day. After six months they can be fed twice daily. Most Labradoodles have healthy appetites and will eat most things put in front of them, it's up to you to control his intake and manage his healthy diet.

Stick to the correct amount. You're

94

doing your pup no favours by overfeeding him. Unless he is particularly thin, don't give in - no matter how much your cute Labradoodle puppy pleads with his big eyes. You must be firm and resist the temptation to give him extra food or treats. Obesity in dogs is one of the main causes of health problems.

Pack leader

Labradoodles are particularly loyal dogs and the person who feeds the puppy will probably become their pack leader. In other words, this is the person to whom the dog will probably show most loyalty and affection. If your dog is not responding well to a particular family member, a useful tactic is to get that person to feed the dog every day. The way to a dog's heart is often through his stomach!

Something else to bear in mind is that if your mealtimes coincide with those of your puppy or adult dog, you should always eat something from your plate before feeding your Labradoodle. Dogs are very hierarchical; they respect the pecking order. In the wild the top dogs eat first. If you feed your puppy before you, he will think that he is higher up the pecking order than you.

If allowed, some Labradoodles can develop a "cocky" attitude and think that they rule the roost. So feeding your dog **after** yourself and your family is an important part of training and discipline. Your dog will not love you any less because you are the boss. In fact, just the opposite.

Feeding Seniors

Once your adolescent Labradoodle has switched to an adult diet he will be on this for most of his life. But as a dog moves towards old age, he begins to slow down and his body has different requirements to those of a

young dog. This is the time to consider switching to a senior diet.

Dogs are living to a much older age than they did 30 years ago. There are many factors contributing to this, including better vaccines and veterinary care, but one of the most important factors is better nutrition. Generally a dog is considered to be 'older' if he is in the last third of his normal life expectancy.

Some owners of large breeds, such as Great Danes with a lifespan of nine years, switch their dogs from an adult to a senior diet when they are only six or seven years old, while other - often smaller - breeds have a longer life expectancy. They may remain relatively youthful for many more years and do not need a senior diet until they are perhaps 10 or older. It all depends on the individual dog, his size, energy levels and general health.

Labradoodles are fairly robust dogs that stay active longer than many breeds. As the Labradoodle is a crossbreed, there are more variables than with a pure breed, but the lifespan of Labradoodles is generally between from around 12 to 15 years. Nine or 10 years is a more common age for Labradoodles to start a senior diet, but it all depends on the individual dog. It may be even later.

Look for signs of your dog slowing down or having joint problems. That may be the time to talk to your vet about moving to a senior diet. You can describe any changes at your dog's annual vaccination appointment, rather than having the expense of a separate consultation.

As a dog grows older, his metabolism slows down, his energy levels decrease and he needs less exercise, just like with humans. You may notice in middle or old age that your dog starts to put weight on. The adult diet he is on may now provide too many calories, so it may be the time to consider switching.

Even though he is older, keep his weight in check as obesity in old age only puts more strain on his body, especially joints and organs, and makes any health problems even worse. Because of lower activity levels, many older dogs will gain weight and getting an older dog to lose weight can be very difficult. It is much better not to let your Labradoodle gain weight than to put him on a diet.

But if he is overweight, put in the effort to slim him down. This is one of the single most important things you can do to increase your dog's quality and length of life.

Other changes in canines are again similar to those in older humans and might include stiff joints or arthritis, moving more slowly and sleeping more. His hearing and vision may not be so sharp and organs don't all work as efficiently as they used to, teeth may have become worn down.

When this starts to happen, it is time to feed your old friend a senior diet, which will take these changes into account. Specially formulated senior diets are lower in calories but help to create a feeling of fullness. Older dogs are more prone to develop constipation, so senior diets are often higher in fibre - at around 3 to 5%.

Wheat bran can also be added to regular dog food to increase the amount of fibre (but do not try this if your Labradoodle has a low tolerance or intolerance to grain). If your dog has poor kidney function, then a low phosphorus diet will help to lower the workload for the kidneys.

Aging dogs have special dietary needs, some of which can be supplied in the form of supplements, such as glucosamine and chondroitin which help joints. If your dog is not eating a complete balanced diet, then a vitamin/mineral supplement is recommended to prevent any deficiencies. Some owners also feed extra antioxidants to an older dog – ask your vet's advice on your next visit. Antioxidants are also found naturally in fruit and vegetables.

While some older dogs suffer from obesity, other have the opposite problem – they lose weight and are disinterested in food. If your dog is getting thin and not eating well, firstly get him checked out by the vet to rule out any possible disease problems. If he gets the all-clear, your next challenge is to tempt him to eat. He may be having trouble with his teeth, so if he's on a dry food, try smaller kibble or moistening it with water. Adding gravy or a small amount of canned food will make it even more appetising.

Some dogs can tolerate a small amount of milk or eggs added to their food, and home-made diets of boiled rice, potatoes, vegetables and chicken or meat with the right vitamin and mineral supplements can also work well.

Reading Dog Food Labels

A NASA scientist would have a hard job understanding some dog food manufacturers' labels, so it's no easy task for us lowly dog owners. Here are some things to look out for on the manufacturers' labels:

Ingredients: Chicken, Chicken By-Product Meal, Corn Meal, Ground Whole Grain Sorghum, Brewers Rice, Ground Whole Grain Barley, Dried Beet Pulp, Chicken Fat (preserved with mixed Tocopherols, a source of Vitamin E), Chicken Flavor, Dried Egg Product, Fish Oil (preserved with mixed Tocopherols, a source of Vitamin E), Potassium Chloride, Salt, Flax Meal, Sodium Hexametaphosphate, Fructooligosaccharides, Choline Chloride, Minerals (Ferrous Sulfate, Zinc Oxide, Manganese Sulfate, Copper Sulfate, Manganous Oxide, Potassium Iodide, Cobalt Carbonate), DL-Methionine, Vitamins (Ascorbic Acid, Vitamin A Acetate, Calcium Pantothenate, Biotin, Thiamine Mononitrate (source of vitamin B1), Vitamin B12 Supplement, Niacin, Riboflavin Supplement (source of vitamin B2), Inositol, Pyridoxine Hydrochloride (source of vitamin B6), Vitamin D3 Supplement, Folic Acid), Calcium Carbonate, Vitamin E Supplement, Brewers Dried Yeast, Beta-Carotene, Rosemary Extract.

* Ingredients are listed by weight and the top one should always be the main content, eg chicken or lamb. Don't pick one where grain is top, it is a poor quality feed and some Labradoodles can develop grain intolerances or allergies, often it is specifically wheat they have a reaction to.

* High up the list should be meat or poultry by-products, these are clean parts of slaughtered animals, not including meat. They include organs, blood and bone, but not hair, horns, teeth or hooves.

* Guaranteed Analysis – This guarantees that your dog's food contains the labelled percentages of crude protein, fat, fibre and moisture. Keep in mind that wet and dry dog foods use different standards. (It does not list the digestibility of protein and fat and this can vary widely depending on their sources). While the guaranteed analysis is a start in understanding the food quality, be wary about relying on it too much.

Crude Protein (min)	32.25%
Lysine (min)	0.43%
Methionine (min)	0.49%
Crude Fat (min)	10.67%
Crude Fiber (max)	7.3%
Calcium (min)	0.50%
Calcium (max)	1.00%
Phosphorus (min)	0.44%
Salt (min)	0.01%
Salt (max)	0.51%

One pet food manufacturer made a mock product with a guaranteed analysis of 10% protein, 6.5% fat, 2.4% fibre, and 68% moisture (similar to what's on many canned pet food labels) – the only problem was that the ingredients were old leather boots, used motor oil, crushed coal and water!

* Chicken meal (dehydrated chicken) has more protein than fresh chicken, which is 80% water. The same goes for beef, fish and lamb. So, if any of these meals are number one on the ingredient list, the food should contain enough protein.

* A certain amount of flavourings can make a food more appetising for your dog. Chose a food with a specific flavouring, like *'beef flavouring'*

rather than a general *'meat flavouring'*, where the origins are not so clear.

* Find a food that fits your dog's age and breed size.

* If your Labradoodle has a food allergy or intolerance to wheat, check whether the food is gluten free. All wheat contains gluten.

* Natural is best. Food labelled *'natural'* means that the ingredients have not been chemically chemical altered, according to the FDA in the USA. However,

there are no such guidelines governing foods labelled "holistic" – so check the ingredients and how it has been prepared.

* In the USA, dog food that meets minimum nutrition requirements has a label that confirms this. It states: **"[food name] is formulated to meet the nutritional levels established by the AAFCO Dog Food Nutrient Profiles for [life stage(s)]".**

Even better, look for a food that meets the minimum nutritional requirements **"as fed"** to real pets in an AAFCO-defined feeding trial, then you know the food really delivers the nutrients that it is "formulated" to. AAFCO feeding trials on real dogs are the gold standard. Brands that do costly feeding trials (including Nestle and Hill's) indicate so on the package.

* Dog food labelled *'supplemental'* isn't complete and balanced. Unless you have a specific, vet-approved need for it, it's not something you want to feed your dog for an extended period of time. Check with your vet if in doubt.

If it still all looks a bit baffling, you might find the following website very useful:
 www.dogfoodadvisor.com run by Mike Sagman. He has a medical background and analyses and rates hundreds of brands of dog food based on the listed ingredients and meat content. You might be surprised at some of his findings.

To recap: no one food is right for every dog. You must decide on the best for your Labradoodle. Once you have decided on a food, monitor your puppy or adult. The best test of a food is how well your dog is doing on it.

If your dog is happy and healthy, interested in life, has enough energy, is not too fat and not too thin, and has healthy-looking stools, then...
Congratulations, you've got it right!

---

6. Training a Labradoodle

Training a Labradoodle is like bringing up a child. Put in the effort early on and you will be rewarded with a well-mannered individual who will be a joy to spend time with for years to come. Labradoodles are intelligent, sociable and playful, but let your youngster do what he wants, allow him to think he's the boss and you may well finish up with mischievous attention-seeking adult.

Too many dogs end up in rescue shelters because they didn't turn out like their owners expected. This is more often than not the owner's fault and lack of training usually played a big part in why the dog developed some unwanted behaviour traits. If you want a dog you can take anywhere and who will be a perfect companion, rather than a pain in the you-know-what, spend time early on teaching him some manners and your rules.

You may consider enlisting the help of a professional trainer, but that option may not be practical or within the budget of some new owners. One excellent alternative is to join a puppy training/behaviour class in your town. This way the pup or adolescent learns with his peers and is socialised with other dogs at the same time.

You could also think about getting a dog training DVD - the beauty of this is that it brings training techniques right into your home – but it should not replace classes with other dogs.

If you train your Doodle yourself, remember the golden rule: training should **always** be based on rewards and not punishment. It is not a battle of wills between you and your dog, it should be a positive learning experience for both. Labradoodles can be sensitive little critters, and bawling at the top of your voice or smacking should play no part in training.

Labradoodles are intelligent and generally regarded as easy to train due to their easy-going temperaments and desire to connect with and please their humans.

They have enquiring minds, most will thrive on training and the chance to exercise their grey matter, even have some fun with it. Some are professionally trained to a very high standard and go on become guide dogs, assistance or therapy dogs.

Over the years, Labradoodles, especially Australian ones, have been bred with a specific easy-going temperament in mind. Early Labradoodles were often headstrong and hyper-active, but well-bred Doodles these days usually have good temperaments and fit well into family life.

That being said, any dog can display bad behaviour if not properly trained. Standard Labradoodles are getting bigger and bigger and if you don't want yours taking you for a walk (instead of the other way round), teach him some good manners and how to walk on the lead without pulling while he is still young, small and willing to learn.

Dogs are pack animals and very hierarchical. They - and you – need to learn their place in the pack and yours is as pack leader. This is not something forced on a dog through shouting and hitting, it is the establishment of the natural order of things by mutual consent and brought about by good training. If not made aware of their place in the household and the rules to abide by, Doodles of all sizes may end up ruling you and your family.

Labradoodles, like most dogs, respect the pecking order and are happy when they know and are comfortable with their place in it. They may push the boundaries, especially as adolescents, but stick to your guns and establish yourself -or family members -as pack leader (or alpha) and the household will run much smoother. Again, this is done with positive techniques, not threats.

Labradoodles are not fierce by nature. The vast majority do not show aggression towards other dogs or humans or bark incessantly. If they do, then you need to nip it in the bud with a bout of firm but fair training.

The first two years are your Doodle's formative years and the most important time for the development of his character and behaviour.

It's your house, you set the rules and with proper training, your Labradoodle will learn to follow them. Be firm, but **never** aggressive with your dog. You will either frighten him or teach him to be aggressive back.

Labradoodles love playing with other dogs and sometimes their concentration may lapse. When giving him a command, you may sometimes see your willing-but-easily-distracted trainee torn between doing what you say or running after that dog/squirrel/human he has just spotted out of the corner of his eye.

Keep training short and fun, especially at the beginning.

If you have adopted an older dog, you can still train him. But it will take a little longer to get rid of bad habits and instil good manners. Patience and persistence are the keys here.

It's relatively easy to train a Labradoodle – it's the owners that take a little longer!

---

14 Top Tips for Training Your Labradoodle

1. **Start training your Labradoodle puppy early.** Like babies, puppies learn quickly and it's this learned behaviour which stays with them through adult life. Old dogs can be taught new tricks, but it's a lot harder to unlearn bad habits. It's best to start training with a clean slate. Puppy training should start with a few minutes a day from Day One when you bring him home, even if he's only a few weeks old.

2. **Your voice is your most important training tool.** Your dog has to learn to understand your language and you have to understand him. Your voice and the tone you employ are very important. Commands should be issued in a calm, authoritative voice - not shouted. Praise should be given in a happy, encouraging voice, accompanied by stroking or patting. If your dog has done something wrong, use a firm, stern voice, not a harsh shriek. This applies even if your Labradoodle is unresponsive at the beginning.

3. **Avoid giving your dog commands you know you can't enforce.** Labradoodles are intelligent dogs. Every time you give a command that you don't enforce, he learns that commands are optional.

4. **Train your dog gently and humanely.** Teach him using positive, motivational methods. Keep training sessions upbeat so the whole experience is enjoyable for you and him. If obedience training is a bit of a bore, pep things up a bit by "play training". Use constructive, non-adversarial games such as Go Find, Hide

and Seek or Fetch.

5. **Begin your training around the house and garden or yard**. How well your dog responds to you at home affects his behaviour away from the home as well. If he doesn't respond well at home, he certainly won't respond any better when he's out and about where there are 101 distractions, such as other dogs, people, food scraps, cats, interesting smells, etc.

6. **One command equals one response.** Give your dog only one command - twice maximum - then gently enforce it. Repeating commands or nagging will make your Labradoodle tune out. They also teach him that the first few commands are a bluff. Telling your dog to **"SIT, SIT, SIT, SIT!!!"** is neither efficient nor effective. Simply give your dog a single "SIT" command, gently place him in the sitting position and then praise him.

7. **It's all about good communication**. It's NOT about getting even with the dog. If you're taking an "it's-me-against-the-dog, I'll soon whip him into shape" approach, you may eventually force your dog into submission. But a relationship based on fear is not a successful one and it will undermine your relationship with him. You'll also miss out on all the fun that a positive training approach can offer.

8. **Use your Labradoodle's name often and in a positive manner.** When you bring your pup or new dog home, start using his name often so he gets used to the sound of it. He won't know what it means in the beginning, but it won't take him long to realise you're talking to him. When training, don't use his name when you are reprimanding, warning or punishing him.

He should trust that when he hears his name, good things happen. His name should always be a word your Doodle responds to with enthusiasm, never hesitancy or fear. Use the words "NO" or "BAD BOY/GIRL" in a stern (not shouted) voice instead. Actually, some people, especially those with children, prefer not to use the word "NO" with their Labradoodle, as it is a word they are using often around the human kids and likely to confuse the canine youngster! You can make a sound like "ACK!" instead. Say it sharply and the dog should stop whatever it is he is doing wrong – this works with our dog, Max.

9. **Don't give your dog lots of attention (even negative**

attention) when he misbehaves. Labradoodles love attention. If he gets lots of attention when he jumps up on you, his bad behaviour is being reinforced. If he jumps up, push him away, use the command "NO" or "DOWN" and then ignore him.

10. **Timing is critical to successful training.** When your puppy does something right, praise him immediately. Similarly, when he does something wrong, correct him straight away. If you don't praise or scold your puppy immediately for something he has done, you cannot do it at all, as he will have no idea what he has done right or wrong.

11. **Have a 'No' sound.** When a puppy is corrected by his mother – for example if he bites her with his sharp baby teeth – she growls at him to warn him not to do it again. When your puppy makes a mistake, make a short sharp sound like **"ACK!"** to tell the puppy not to do that again. This works surprisingly well.

12. **Be patient.** Rome wasn't built in a day and a Labradoodle won't be trained in 24 hours either. But you'll reap the rewards of a few weeks of regular training sessions for the rest of the dog's life when you have a happy, well-behaved friend and loving companion for life.

13. **Give your dog attention when YOU want to** – not when he wants it. Labradoodles are sociable creatures, they love being with you and involved with the family. When you are training, it is good to give your puppy lots of positive attention when he is good. But if he starts jumping up, nudging you constantly or barking to demand your attention, ignore him. If you give in to his every demand, he will start to think he is the boss and become more demanding. Wait a while and pat him when you want and when he has stopped demanding your attention.

14. **Start as you mean to go on.** In other words, in terms of rules and training, treat your fluffy little Doodle pup as though he were fully grown: make him abide by the rules you want him to live by as an adult. If you don't want him to take over your couch or jump up at people when he is big,

don't allow him to do it when he is small. You can't have one set of rules for pups and one set for adult dogs, they won't understand.

Starting Off on the Right Foot

Despite what you may think, training a Labradoodle can be a pleasure of toil. Properly done it is a rewarding experience, a learning curve and a lot of fun - for both you and your dog.

No matter how easy-to-please your dog is, obedience training is an absolute must for every dog. Most Doodles are pretty smart and have a fairly low boredom threshold. As they get grow and get more confident in their new surroundings, they may try to push the boundaries and jump up at people, ignore your call or sit on your comfy sofa - if you'll let them. This may happen particularly around adolescence - between a few months and two years old.

If you allow them to get away with these and other bad habits, this poor behaviour will soon become ingrained - Doodles soon work out what is and what is not permitted and if you don't want yours to become a pest, start your training early and stick with it.

Labradoodles love to be at the centre of life, many are attention seekers. They are also enthusiastic and eager to please, two main reasons why they generally respond well to training. Praise for a job well done has a powerful effect on them during training. Like most dogs, they don't respond well to negative reinforcement, which only increases stress and anxiety.

Without discipline and guidelines, the Doodle's energy and playfulness can occasionally turn to stubbornness. Some dogs, just like children, will act up in order to get attention. What often happens is that the owner starts to shout, so he soon realises that shouting means he gets attention, which makes his behaviour even worse.

If your dog tries it on, you should:

- Make a fuss of him for good behaviour
- Ignore bad behaviour – however difficult this might be

When he sees that he gets all the attention for being a good boy and none when he is naughty, his behaviour should improve.

Many Doodles have a short attention span. When training he may be tempted to wander off to sniff or follow something more interesting than you. The key to successful training is **variety** rather than repetition, keep training interesting and fun. Too much repetition will cause him to get bored and lose concentration.

Routine

Training your Labradoodle is a must-do. A well-behaved dog you can take anywhere without worrying is a marvellous companion. Try and do a little bit every day, starting with a few minutes a day with a new puppy, and once your dog has learned good behaviour, reinforce it every now and again on your walks, rewarding him with an occasional treat. Training doesn't stop because a dog grows up, he continues to learn throughout his life.

If you start your training early enough, and then take a few minutes in your normal daily routine to reinforce what your dog has learned, you'll end up with a wonderful companion that is not only well-behaved but also the envy of all your friends.

Some Basic Training

Sit

Teaching the sit command to your Doodle is a doddle. Teaching him to sit still is a bit more difficult! You may want to put your pup on a lead (leash) to hold his attention in the beginning.

1. Stand facing each other and hold a treat a few inches above his head (By the way, it's rather pointless paying for a high quality, possibly hypoallergenic dog food and then filling him with trashy treats. Buy premium treats with natural ingredients which won't cause allergies.)
2. As he reaches up to sniff it, move the treat upwards and back over the dog towards his tail at the same time as saying "Sit".
3. As his head moves up toward the treat, his rear end should automatically go down towards the floor.
4. As soon as he sits, give him the treat and tell your dog (s)he's a good boy/girl. Stroke and praise him for as long as he stays in the sitting position.
5. Practice it in short sessions until he does it every time. After a while, he should do it just from command, without moving the treat over him. When he does, give him a treat anyway.

If he jumps up on his back legs and paws you while you are moving the treat, be patient and start all over again. Another method is to put one hand on his chest and with your other hand, gently push down on his rear end until he is sitting, while saying "Sit". Give him a treat and praise, even though you have made him do it, he will eventually associate the position with the word 'sit'.

'Sit' is a useful command and can be used in a number of different situations. For example when you are putting his lead on, while you are preparing his meal, when he returned the ball you have just thrown, when he is demanding attention or getting over-excited.

Preventing puppy biting

Play biting is normal for puppies, they do it all the time with their siblings in the litter. They bite moving targets with their sharp teeth; it's a great game. But when they arrive in your home, they have to be taught that human body parts are not suitable material for biting.

Try not to encourage play-biting. As a puppy grows and feels more confident in his surroundings, he may become slightly more aggressive and his bites may hurt someone – especially if you have children or elderly people at home. Make sure every time you have a play session you have a soft toy nearby and when he starts to chew your hand or feet, clench your fingers (or toes!) to make it more difficult and distract him with a soft toy in your other hand.

Keep the game interesting by moving the toy around or rolling it around in front of him. (He may be too young to fetch it back if you throw it.) He may continue to chew you, but will eventually realise that the toy is far more interesting and lively than your boring hand.

If he becomes over-excited and too aggressive with the toy, if he growls a lot, stop playing with him and **walk away**. Although it might be quite cute and funny now, you don't want him doing this as an adult. Remember, if not checked, any unwanted behaviour traits will continue into adulthood, when you certainly don't want him to bite your children's hands or growl at them.

When you walk away, don't say anything or make eye or physical contact with your puppy. Simply ignore him, this is extremely effective and often works within a few days.

If your pup is more persistent and tries to bite your legs as you walk away, thinking this is another fantastic game, stand still and ignore him.

If he still persists, tell him "NO" in a very stern voice, then praise him when he lets go.

Many Labradoodles are very intuitive and another method which can be very successful is to make a sharp cry of **"Ouch!"** when your pup bites your hand – even when it doesn't hurt. This worked very well for us. Your pup may well jump back in amazement, surprised that he has hurt you.

Divert your attention from your puppy to your hand. He will probably try to get your attention or lick you as a way of saying sorry. Praise him for stopping biting and continue with the game. If he bites you again, repeat the process. A sensitive dog will soon stop biting you.

It might be an idea to keep the toys you use to play with the puppy separate from other toys he may have. That way he will associate certain toys with having fun with you and will work harder to please you.

Top 10 Tips for Housetraining

The good news is that a dog's instinct is not to soil his own den. From about the age of three weeks, a puppy will leave his sleeping area to go to the toilet. The bad news is that when you bring your little pup home, he doesn't realise that the whole house is his den. Therefore you need to teach him that it is unacceptable to make a mess anywhere inside the house.

How long this takes depends on how quickly your dog learns and how persistent and patient you are. It could take from a few days to several months.

Follow these tips to speed up the process:

1. **Constant supervision** for the first week or two is essential if you are to housetrain your puppy quickly. This is why it is important to book the week off work when you bring a new puppy home. Making sure you are there to take him outside regularly is very important. If nobody is there, he will learn to urinate or poo(p) inside the house

2. Take your puppy outside to **the same place** every time. Dogs naturally develop a preference for going in the same spot or on the same surface -often grass. Take him to the same patch every time so he learns this is his toilet - preferably an area in a far corner or your garden or yard.

3. **No pressure – be patient** You must allow your Doodle pup the time to wander around and have a good sniff before performing his duties – but do not leave him, stay around a short distance away. Sadly, puppies are not known for their powers of concentration. They may become easily distracted and it may take a while for them to select that perfect spot to wee (pee) on!

4. **Share the responsibility.** It doesn't have to be the same person that takes the dog outside all the time. In fact it's easier if there are a couple of you, as housetraining a pup is a very time-consuming business. Just make sure you stick to the same routines and patch of ground.

5. **Take your pup outside at the following times:**
   a. As soon as he wakes – every time
   b. Shortly after each feed
   c. After a drink
   d. When he gets excited
   e. After exercise or play
   f. Last thing at night
   g. Initially every hour – whether or not he looks like he wants to go.

6. **Stick to the same routine.** Dogs understand and like routine. Sticking to the same one for meal times, short exercise sessions, play time, sleeping and toilet breaks will help to not only housetrain him quicker, but help him settle into his new home.

7. **Shout if you catch him in the act indoors.** A short sharp negative sound is best - No! Ack! Eh! - it doesn't matter so long as it is loud enough to make him stop. Then start running enthusiastically towards your door, calling him into the garden and the chosen spot and patiently wait until he has finished what he started indoors.

8. **No punishment.** Accidents will happen at the beginning, do not punish your dog for them. He is a baby with a tiny bladder and bowels and housetraining takes time - it is perfectly natural to have accidents early on. Remain calm and clean up the mess with a good strong-smelling cleaner to remove the odour, so he won't be tempted to use that spot again.

Dogs have a very strong sense of smell and to make 100% sure there is no trace of what they left behind, you can use a special spray from your vet or a hot solution of washing powder to completely eliminate the odour. Smacking or rubbing his nose in it can have the opposite effect, he will become afraid to do his business in your presence and may start going behind the couch or under the bed, rather than in the garden. Only shout if you catch him in the act, never afterwards.

9. **Look for the signs.** These may be sniffing the floor in a determined manner, circling looking for a place to go or walking uncomfortably, particularly at the rear end. Take him outside straight away. **Do not pick him up**, he has to learn to walk to the door himself as a signal that he needs to go outside.

10. **Housetraining is reward-based.** Praise him or give him a treat when he performs his duties in the chosen spot. Labradoodles love treats as well as pleasing their owners. Reward-based training is the most successful method.

You may also want to use a trigger to encourage your dog to perform his duties; they can be very effective. Some people use a clicker or a bell, we used a word. In a relatively short space of time, we trained Max to urinate on the command of "wee wee." Think carefully before choosing the word or phrase, as I often feel an idiot wandering around our garden last thing at night shouting "Max, wee wee" in an encouraging manner!

7. Labradoodle Behaviour

Treated well and exercised daily, Labradoodles make wonderful family pets. That's one of the reasons why so many owners get a second Labradoodle - or even more. Once smitten, never forgotten.

Some owners would say that Labradoodles regard themselves as part of the household. They are certainly very sociable animals and enjoy being with people and taking part in their daily lives. But sometimes dogs can develop behaviour problems – even Doodles! There are numerous reasons why a dog might behave badly, every dog is an individual and every case is different.

Cause and Effect
Poor behaviour may result from a number of factors, including:

- Poor breeding
- Being badly treated
- Boredom due to lack of exercise
- Being left alone too long
- A change in living conditions
- Anxiety or insecurity
- Lack of socialisation
- Fear

Bad behaviour may show itself in a number of different ways, such as:

- Chewing or destructive behaviour
- Barking
- Nipping
- Biting
- Jumping up
- Soiling or urinating inside the house
- Growling at people
- Aggression towards other dogs

In this chapter, we look at some of the more familiar behaviour problems. Although every dog is different and requires individual assessment and treatment, we outline some common causes of bad behaviour and offer general pointers to help improve the situation if there is a problem. The best way to avoid it is to put in the time early on to train your dog and nip any potential problems in the bud. This isn't always possible if, for example, you are rehoming a dog, when more time and patience will be needed.

Whatever the causes, if the bad behaviour persists, you should consider consulting a canine professional.

Personality

Just like humans, a dog's personality is made up of a combination of temperament and character. **Temperament** is the nature the dog is born with and it is inherited.

This is why getting your puppy from a good breeder is so important. Not only will a responsible breeder produce puppies from physically healthy dams and sires, but they will also look at the temperament of their dogs and only breed from those with good temperament traits.

Character is what develops through the dog's life and is formed by a combination of temperament and environment. How the dog is treated will have a great effect on his or her personality and behaviour.

Starting off on the right foot with good routines and training for your puppy is very important. Treat your dog well, spend time with him or her, exercise regularly, praise good behaviour and be firm when he or she needs discipline. These measures will all help your Labradoodle to grow into a happy, well-adjusted and well-behaved adult dog.

If you adopt a rescue Labradoodle, you may need a little extra patience. These people-loving dogs may arrive with some baggage. They have been abandoned by their previous owners for a variety of reasons and some still carry the scars of that trauma. They may feel insecure or fearful. Your time and patience is needed to teach these dogs to trust again and to become happy in their new forever homes.

Top 10 Ways to Avoid Bad Behaviour

Different dogs have different reasons for exhibiting bad behaviour. There is no simple cure for everything. Your best chance of ensuring your Labradoodle does not become badly behaved is to start out on the right foot and follow these simple guidelines:

1. **Buy from a good breeder**. A good breeder will only breed Labradoodles. They will use their expertise to match suitable breeding couples, taking into

account factors such as good temperament and health.

2. **Start training early.** You can't start too soon, like babies, puppies have enquiring minds which can quickly absorb a lot of new information. You can start teaching your puppy to learn his own name a well as some simple commands from as early as two months old.

3. **Basic training should cover several areas:** housetraining, chew prevention, puppy biting, simple commands like sit, come, stay and familiarising him with a collar and lead. Adopt a gentle approach when your dog is young. He will lose attention and get frightened if you are too harsh. Start with five to 10 minutes a day and build up. Often the way a dog responds to his or her environment is a result of owner training and management – or lack of it.

4. **Take the time to learn what sort of temperament your dog has** – and train him accordingly. Is he by nature a nervous type or a confident chap? What was he like as a puppy, did he rush forward or hang back? Did he fight to get upright when you turned him on his back or was he happy to lie there? Your puppy's temperament will affect his behaviour and how he reacts to the world around him. A timid Labradoodle will not respond well to being shouted at, whereas a dominant, boisterous one will need more effort on your part as well as more discipline and exercise.

5. **Socialise your dog with other dogs and people.** Lack of interaction with people and other canines is one of the major causes of bad behaviour. Puppy classes or adult dog obedience classes are a great way to start, but make sure you do your homework afterwards. Spend a few minutes each day reinforcing what you have both learned in class. Owners need training as well as Labradoodles!

Socialisation does not end at puppyhood. Dogs are social creatures that thrive on seeing, smelling and even licking their fellow canines. While the foundation for good behaviour is laid down during the first few months, good owners will reinforce social skills and training throughout a dog's life.

Exposing your dog to different kinds of people, animals and environments - from dog obedience classes to visits to the vet and walks in the park - helps him develop confidence and ease. This goes a long way in helping a dog become a more stable, happy and trustworthy companion and reduces his chances of developing unwanted behaviour traits.

6. **Lots of exercise.** A lack of exercise is another main reason why dogs behave badly, especially Standard Labradoodles, which are athletic dogs. All three types of Labradoodle are intelligent and a lack of mental and physical stimulation can result in poor behaviour, such as excessive barking, chewing or ignoring commands as the dog becomes bored or frustrated.
    A tired Labradoodle is a happy Labradoodle, see **Chapter 8. Exercise** on how much daily exercise your Labradoodle needs outside the home.

7. **Reward your dog for good behaviour.** All training should be based on positive reinforcement; praising and rewarding your dog when he does something good, like responding to a command. Generally Labradoodles are keen to please their owners, but can resort to bad behaviour when the boundaries are not set. The main aims of training are to build a better relationship between your dog and you, the master, and to make him feel secure. Dogs often become stubborn and don't obey commands when there is not much interaction between them and their owners. Make sure you take the time to train him and tell him what a good boy he is when he behaves well.

8. **Ignore bad behaviour**, no matter how hard this may be. If, for example, he is chewing his or way through your kitchen units, couch or plasterboard walls, remove your dog from the situation and then ignore him. For some dogs even negative attention such as shouting is some attention. The more time you spend praising and rewarding good behaviour while ignoring bad behaviour, the more likely he is to respond to you.

9. **Learn to leave your dog.** Just as leaving your dog alone for too long can lead to behaviour problems, so can being with him 100% of the time. The dog becomes over-reliant on his owner and then gets stressed when left. This is known as separation anxiety and usually results in the dog barking or whining incessantly when separated from his owner. It is a stressful situation for both owner and dog. When your dog is a puppy, or when he arrives at your house as an adult, start by leaving him for a few minutes every

day and gradually build it up so that after a few weeks or months you can leave him for up to four hours. See our sections on **Separation Anxiety** later in this chapter.

10. **Love your dog – but don't spoil him.** Smaller dogs can develop into 'Little Emperors,' while Standard Labradoodles can become over-boisterous and hard to control if allowed to rule the roost. This may result in them becoming stubborn and ignoring your commands, or resorting to barking, growling, jumping up or nipping if they think that they are in charge. On the other hand, you don't do your dog any favours by giving him too many treats. Obesity can be a contributory factor to a number of health problems, including diabetes and bladder stones.

Dogs don't just suddenly start behaving badly for no reason. As with humans, there's usually a trigger. Get to know the temperament of Labradoodles in general and your own dog's individual personality and build up a loving, trusting relationship.

Excessive barking

Some puppies start off by being noisy from the outset ,while others hardly bark at all until they reach adolescence or adulthood. On our website we get emails from dog owners worried that their young pets are not barking enough. However, we get many more from owners whose dogs are barking too much!

Although not normally noisy dogs, Labradoodles are generally good watchdogs, and barking is their way of alerting their owners of the arrival of other people or animals - whether friend or foe. As humans, we use can use our voice in many different ways: to express happiness or anger, to scold, to shout a warning, and so on. Dogs are the same; different barks give out different messages. A very high pitched bark may indicate fear.

To start out with, when your dog barks at an arrival at your house, gently praise him after the first few barks. If he persists, gently tell him that that is enough. Like humans, some dogs can get carried away with the sound of their own voice, so try and discourage too much barking from the outset.

Excessive, habitual barking is a problem which should be corrected early on before it gets out of hand and drives you and your neighbours nuts.

The problem often develops during adolescence or early adulthood as the dog becomes more confident.

Listen to your dog and try and distinguish the different meanings. A dog does not have different words to express himself, he has to rely on the tone of his bark. Learn to recognise the difference between an alert bark, an excited bark, an aggressive bark or a plain "I'm barking coz I can" bark.

Your behaviour can also encourage a dog to bark excessively. If your dog barks non-stop for several minutes and then you give him a treat to quieten him, he will associate his barking with getting a nice treat and keep doing it.

A better way to deal with it is to say in a firm voice "Quiet" after he has made a few barks. When he stops, praise him and he will get the idea that what you want him to do is stop. The trick is to nip the bad behaviour in the bud before it becomes an ingrained habit.

Speak and Shush!

One technique is the Speak and Shush technique where you teach your dog or puppy to bark and be quiet on command. Get a friend to stand outside your front door and say "Speak" (or "Woof" or "Alert"). This is the cue for your accomplice to knock or ring the bell.

When your dog barks, praise him profusely. You can even bark yourself to encourage the dog! After a few good barks, say "Shush" and then dangle

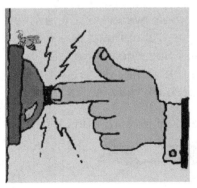

a tasty treat in front of his nose. He will stop barking as soon as he sniffs the treat, because it is impossible to sniff and woof at the same time.

Praise your dog again as he sniffs quietly and then give him the treat. Repeat this routine a few times a day and your dog will learn to bark whenever the doorbell rings and you ask him to speak. Eventually your dog will bark after your request but BEFORE the doorbell rings, meaning he has learned to bark on command. Even better, he will learn to anticipate the likelihood of getting a treat following your "Shush" request and will also be quiet on command.

With Speak and Shush training, progressively increase the length of required shush time before offering a treat - at first just a couple of seconds, then three, five, ten, twenty and so on. By alternating instructions to speak and shush, the dog is praised and rewarded for barking on request and also for stopping barking on request.

Always use your favourite teacher voice when training, speak softly when instructing your dog to shush, and reinforce the shush with whisper-praise. The more softly you speak, the more your dog will be likely to pay attention.

Aggression

Some breeds are more prone to be aggressive than others. Fortunately, this is a problem not often seen in Labradoodles, as they are generally non-aggressive by nature. However, given a certain set of circumstances, any dog can growl or bite. If your dog does show these tendencies, you have to find the cause before you can find the remedy.

One of the most common triggers is fear. This fear often comes from a bad experience the dog has suffered or from lack of proper socialisation. Another form of fear-aggression is when a dog becomes over-protective of his owner.

An owner's treatment of a dog can be another reason. If the owner has been too harsh with the dog, such as shouting, using physical violence or reprimanding the dog too often, this can cause the dog to become aggressive. Again this is fuelled by fear. Dogs can also become aggressive if they are consistently chained, under-fed or under-exercised. A bad experience with another dog or dogs can be a further cause.

Many dogs are more combative on the lead (leash). This is because once on a lead, they cannot run away and escape. They therefore become more aggressive, barking or growling to warn off the other dog or person. The dog knows he can't run off, so tries to make himself as frightening as possible.

Socialising your puppy when young is very important. Many dog trainers believe that the first six months of a puppy's life is the critical time for socialisation and during that early period they should be introduced to as many different situations, people and dogs as possible.

Techniques

Teaching your dog what is unacceptable behaviour in the first place is the best preventative measure. Early training, especially during puppy years and before he or she develops the habit of biting, can save a lot of trouble in the future. Professional dog trainers employ a variety of techniques with a dog which has become aggressive. Firstly they will look at the causes and then they almost always use reward-based methods to try and cure fearful or aggressive dogs.

Counter conditioning is a positive training technique used by many professional trainers to help change a dog's aggressive behaviour towards other dogs. A typical example would be a dog which snarls, barks and lunges at other dogs while on the leash. It is the presence of other dogs which is triggering the dog to act in a fearful or anxious manner.

Every time the dog sees another dog, he or she is given a tasty treat to counter the aggression. With enough steady repetition, the dog starts to associate the presence of other dogs with a tasty treat. Properly and patiently done (it won't happen overnight), the final result is a dog which calmly looks to the owner for the treat whenever he or she sees another dog while on the leash.

Whenever you encounter a potentially aggressive situation, divert your dog's attention by turning his head away from the other dog and towards you, so that he cannot make eye contact with the other dog.

Aggression Towards People
In evolutionary terms, it is not that long ago that dogs were wild creatures, living in packs, hunting for food and defending themselves and their territory against potential enemies.

For today's dog, aggression toward people is born out of fear and surfaces as a result of a real or perceived threat. The classic example is of a person who walks straight up to a dog, stares him in the eyes and pats him on top of his head. To the dog, each one of those actions suggests confrontation.

The person might be communicating: "Hey, how are you?" But the dog may read the human behaviour as dangerous and an attempt to dominate. It is not the dog's fault, he is reacting instinctively to a given situation. However, it is not acceptable for a dog to attack people, so he must learn to stop this behaviour.

If your dog doesn't like people or is afraid of them, you need to find a way to instil confidence. When somebody comes to your house or into the garden or yard, your dog needs to feel that this is a friend, not an enemy. If you have regular delivery person or postman that your dog takes a dislike to, some behaviourists recommend having treats available that the person gave give to your dog to try and gain his trust.

If your dog is persistently aggressive towards people, this behaviour must be dealt with and we recommend calling in a professional dog trainer or behaviourist.

Techniques

Desensitisation is the most common method of treating aggression. It starts by breaking down the triggers for the behaviour one small step at a time. The aim is to get the dog to associate pleasant things with the trigger, i.e. people or a specific person which he previously feared or regarded as a threat.

This is done through using positive reinforcement, such as praise or treats. Successful desensitisation takes time, patience and knowledge. Again, a professional behaviourist will give you detailed instructions at the outset. If your dog is starting to growl or snarl at people, there are a couple of techniques you can try to break him of this bad habit before it develops into full-blown biting.

One method is to arrange for some friends to come round, one at a time. When they arrive at your house, get them to scatter kibble on the floor in front of them so that your dog associates the arrival of people with tasty treats. As they move into the house, and your dog eats the kibble, praise your canine for being a good boy. Manage your dog's environment. Don't over-face him. If he's at all anxious around children, manage him carefully around them or avoid them altogether. Children typically react to dogs enthusiastically and some dogs may regard this as an invasion of their space.

Some canines are aggressive towards the partner of a dog owner. Several people have written to our website about this and it usually involves a male partner or husband and a small dog. Often the dog is jealous of the attention his owner is giving to the man, or it could be that the dog feels threatened by him.

They key here is for the partner to gradually gain the trust of the dog. He or she should show that they are not a threat by speaking gently to the dog and giving treats when the dog is well behaved. Avoid eye contact, as the dog may perceive this as a challenge.

If the subject of the dog's aggression lives in the house, then try letting this person give the dog his daily feeds. The way to a dog's heart is often through his stomach.

Coprophagia (Eating Faeces)

It is hard for us to understand why a dog would want to eat his or any other animal's faces, but it does happen. Nobody fully understands why dogs do this, it may simply be an unpleasant behaviour trait or there could be an underlying reason.

If your dog eats faces from the cat litter tray (a problem several owners have contacted us about), the first thing to do is to place the litter tray somewhere where the dog can't get to it – but the cat can. Perhaps on a shelf or put a guard around it, small enough for the cat to get through but not your Labradoodle.

Our dog sometimes eats cow or horse manure when out in the countryside. He usually stops when we tell him to and he hasn't suffered any after effects – so far.

Vets have found that canine diets with low levels of fibre and high levels of starch increase the likelihood of coprophagia. If your dog is exhibiting this behaviour, first check that the diet you are feeding is nutritionally complete. Look at the first ingredient on the dog food packet or tin – is it corn or meat? Does he look skinny? Check that you are feeding him enough.

If there is no underlying medical reason, then you will have to modify your dog's behaviour. Remove cat litter trays, clean up after your dog and do not allow him to eat his own faeces. If it's not there, he can't eat it. Don't reprimand the dog for this behaviour. A better technique is to distract him while he is in the act and then remove the offending material.

Coprophagia is usually seen in pups between six months to a year old and often disappears after this age.

———————

Separation Anxiety

It's not just Labradoodles that experience separation anxiety - people do too. About 7% of adults and 4% of children suffer from this disorder. Typical symptoms for humans are:

- distress at being separated from a loved one
- fear of being left alone

Our canine companions aren't much different to us. When a dog leaves the litter, his owners become his new family or pack.

It's estimated that as many as 10% to 15% of dogs suffer from separation anxiety. All three types of Labradoodle are susceptible because they thrive on interaction with people and generally do not do well if left alone for long periods.

Separation anxiety is on the increase and recognised by behaviourists as the most common form of stress for dogs. Millions of dogs suffer from it.

Distressing

It can be equally distressing for the owner - I know because Max suffers from this. He howls whenever we leave home without him. Fortunately his

problem is only a mild one. If we return after only a short while, he's usually quiet. Although if we silently sneak back home and peek in through the letterbox, he's never asleep. Instead he's waiting by the door looking and listening for our return.

It can be embarrassing. Whenever I go to the Post Office, I tie him up outside and even though he can see me through the glass door, he still barks his head off - so loud that the people inside can't make themselves heard. Luckily the lady behind the counter is a dog lover and, despite the large **'GUIDE DOGS ONLY'** sign outside, she lets Max in. He promptly dashes through the door, sits down beside me and stays quiet as a mouse!

Tell-Tale Signs

Does your Labradoodle do any of the following -

- Dig, chew, or scratch at doors and windows trying to join you?
- Tear up paper or chew cushions, couches and other furniture?

- Howl, bark or cry in an attempt to get you to return?
- Foul inside the house, even though he is housetrained? (This **only** occurs when left alone).
- Follow you from room to room whenever you're home?
- Exhibit restlessness - such as licking his coat excessively, pacing or circling?
- Greet you ecstatically every time you come home – even if you've only been out to empty the trash?
- Get anxious or stressed when you're getting ready to leave the house?
- Dislike spending time outdoors alone?

If so, he or she may suffer from separation anxiety. Fortunately, in many cases, this can be cured.

Canine Separation Anxiety in Puppies

This is fairly common, dogs are pack animals and it is not natural for them to be alone. Puppies need to be patiently taught to get used to isolation slowly and in a structured way if they are to be comfortable with it.

A puppy will emotionally latch on to his new owner who has taken the place of his mother and siblings. He will want to follow you everywhere initially and although you want to shower him with love and attention, it's important to leave your new puppy alone for short periods in the beginning and then later on to avoid him becoming totally dependent on you.

Adopted dogs may be particularly susceptible to separation anxiety. They may have been abandoned once already and fear it happening again.

I was working from home when we got Max. With hindsight, it would have been better if we'd regularly left him alone for a couple of hours more often in the first few months.

Symptoms are not commonly seen in middle-aged dogs, although dogs that develop symptoms when young may be at risk later on. Separation anxiety is, however, common in elderly dogs.

Pets age and - like humans - their senses, such as hearing and sight, deteriorate. They become more dependent on their owners and may then become more anxious when they are separated from them - or even out of view.

It may be very flattering and cute that your dog wants to be with you all the time, but it is an insecurity and separation anxiety is a form of panic, which is distressing for your dog. If he shows any signs, help him to become more self-reliant and confident; he will be a happier dog.

So what can you do if your dog is showing signs of canine separation anxiety? Every dog is different, but here are tried and tested techniques which have proved effective for some dogs.

Eight Tips to Reduce Separation Anxiety

1. Exercise. Tire your dog out before you leave him alone. Take him for a long walk or play a game until he runs out of steam. When you leave the house he'll be too tired to make a big fuss.

2. Keep arrivals and departures low key. Don't make a big fuss when you go out or when you come home. For example when I come home, Max is hysterically happy and runs round whimpering with a toy in his mouth. I make him sit and stay and then let him out into the garden without patting or acknowledging him. I pat him several minutes later.

3. Leave your dog a "security blanket" such as an old piece of clothing you have recently worn which still has your scent on it.

4. Leave a radio on - but not too loud - in the room with the dog so he doesn't feel so alone. Try and avoid a heavy rock station! If it will be dark when you return, leave a lamp on a timer.

5. Associate your departure with something good. As you leave, give your dog a rubber toy like a Kong filled with a tasty treat. This may take his mind off of your departure. We've tried this with Max, but he "punishes" us by refusing to touch the treat until we return home -and then he wolfs it down.

6. If your dog is used to a crate, then try crating him when you go out. Many dogs feel safe there, and

being in a crate can also help to reduce their destructiveness. Always take his collar off first. Pretend to leave the house, but listen for a few minutes. A word of warning – if your dog starts to show major signs of distress, remove him from the crate immediately as he may injure himself.

7. Counter-conditioning. This involves tiny, gradual departures which teach your dog to be alone for gradually longer periods of time. (See Sit-Stay-Down below.)

8. Dogs read body language very well and many Labradoodles are particularly intuitive. They may start to fret when they think you are going to leave them. One technique is to mimic your departure routine when you have no intention of leaving. So put your coat on, grab your car keys, go out of the door and return a few seconds later. Do this randomly and regularly and it may help to reduce your dog's stress levels when you do them for real.

In severe cases, the dog may require medication from a qualified vet. Before this happens, the dog needs a thorough history and medical examination to rule out any other behavioural problems or illnesses.

Sit-Stay-Down
Another technique for reducing separation anxiety in dogs is to practice the common "sit-stay" or "down-stay" training exercises using positive reinforcement.

The goal is to be able to move briefly out of your dog's sight while he is in the "stay" position. Through this your dog learns that he can remain calmly and happily in one place while you go about your normal daily life.

You have to progress extremely slowly with this and much patience is needed, it may take weeks or even months. Get your dog to sit and stay

and then walk away from him for five seconds, then 10, 15 and so on, gradually increase the distance you move away from your dog. Reward your dog with a treat every time he stays calm.

Then move out of sight or out of the room for a few seconds, return and give him the treat if he is calm, gradually lengthen the time you are out of sight. If you're watching TV with the dog by your side and you get up for a snack, tell him to stay and leave the room. When you come back, give him a treat or praise him quietly.

It is a good idea to practice these techniques after exercise or when your dog is sleepy, as he is likely to be more relaxed.

What You Must Never Do

Canine Separation Anxiety is NOT the result of disobedience or lack of training. It's a psychological condition, your dog feels anxious and insecure.

NEVER punish your dog for showing signs of separation anxiety – even if he has chewed your best couch. This will only make him worse.

NEVER leave your dog in a crate if he is frantic to get out. It may cause him physical or mental harm.

Important: This chapter provides only a general overview of dog behaviour. If your dog does have behaviour problems, particularly if he or she is aggressive towards people or other dogs, you should seek help from a reputable canine behaviourist.

8. Exercise

Benefits of Regular Exercise

One thing all dogs – including every Labradoodle ever born - have in common is that they need daily exercise and the best way to give them this is by regular walks. Here is what daily exercise does for your dog - and you:

- Strengthens respiratory and circulatory systems
- Helps get oxygen to tissue cells
- Wards off obesity
- Keeps muscles toned and joints flexible
- Helps digestion

Whether you live in an apartment or on a farm, start regular exercise and feeding patterns early so the dog gets used and adapts to his and your daily routine.

Daily exercise helps to keep your dog healthy, happy and free from disease.

How Much Exercise?

Labradoodles are generally regarded as having medium exercise requirements. There is no one-rule-fits-all solution, the amount of exercise that each individual dog needs varies tremendously. It depends on a number of issues, including size, temperament, his natural energy levels, your living conditions, whether he is kept with other dogs and, importantly, what he gets used to.

Veterinarians advise that you take your Labradoodle out for at least one decent walk every day - and two or three times daily is even better. At least 30 minutes a day is the **minimum** recommended exercise for a Miniature Labradoodle while a large one needs at least an hour or more. Labradoodles are not slothful by nature and a fenced garden or yard where they can burn off some energy between walks is an advantage, but should never be seen as a replacement for daily walks.

You shouldn't think about getting a Labradoodle - or any other type of dog - if you cannot commit to at least one walk every day with your dog

It's good practice to establish an exercise regime early in the dog's life. Dogs like routine, but remember there are strict guidelines to stick to with

126

puppies – see our section later in this chapter. It is important not to over-exercise them, particularly with large breeds and crossbreeds like the Standard Labradoodle.

Their bones and joints are developing and cannot tolerate a great deal of stress, so playing Frisbee for hours on end with your adolescent or puppy Labradoodle is not a good option. You'll end up with a damaged dog and a pile of veterinary bills.

Establish a Routine

What is a good idea, however, is to get the dog used to exercise at the  same time every day at a time that fits in with your daily routine. For example, taking the dog out after his morning feed, then perhaps a longer walk in the afternoon or when you come home from work, and a short toilet trip last thing at night.

Daily exercise could mean a walk around the block, jogging on the bike path, playing fetch the ball or swimming, an activity loved by most Labradoodles.

Swimming is a great way for dogs to exercise, so much so that many veterinary practices are not incorporating small water tanks, not only for remedial therapy, but also for canine recreation. Many Labradoodles will dash in and out of the water all day if you'll let them, but remember that swimming is a lot more strenuous and tiring for your dog than walking, so don't over-stretch him.

Whatever routine you decide on, your dog should be getting out on a walk at least once a day (preferably more) and you should stick to it. If you begin by taking your Doodle out three times a day and then suddenly stop, he will become restless and attention-seeking because he has been used to having more exercise.

Conversely, don't expect a dog used to little exercise to suddenly go on day-long hikes, he will probably struggle. Medium and larger Labradoodles may make suitable hiking or jogging companions, but they need to build up gradually to that amount of exercise - and such strenuous activity is not suitable for puppies.

To those owners who say their dog is happy and getting enough exercise playing in the yard or garden, just show him his lead (leash) and see how he reacts. Do you think he is excited at the prospect of leaving the property and going for a walk? Of course he is. Nothing can compensate for all the interesting smells in the park, meeting other dogs, playing games or going swimming. Labradoodles generally have a great sense of fun and love all these activities.

If you have a busy life and can only take your Doodle out once a day, get into the routine early on. This will help your dog's body and mind to adjust to your lifestyle. Look on the bright side, a brisk walk is a great way of keeping both you and your dog fit – even when it's raining or snowing. In fact, many Labradoodles love snow.

Don't think that as your dog gets older, he won't need exercising. Older dogs need exercise to keep their body, joints and systems functioning properly. They need a less strenuous regime than younger dogs, but still enough to keep them active, alert and healthy as well as mentally stimulated. Regular exercise can add months or even years to a dog's life.

Physical and Mental Stimulation
Labradoodles need sufficient exercise for their physical wellbeing – heart, muscles and joints – but also for their mental wellbeing. They are intelligent dogs and without sufficient exercise can become bored and restless. This can result in behavioural and attention-seeking problems, and some of them may become destructive.
It is important to exercise a Labradood**le's mind as well as his body.** It used to be that experts recommended starting training when your dog was one year old, but modern thinking has changed. You can start training your Labradoodle from the day you bring him home, even from as early as eight weeks.

If your Labradoodle's behaviour deteriorates or he suddenly starts chewing things he's not supposed to, the first question you should ask yourself is: "Is he getting enough exercise?" Boredom through lack of exercise or stimulation (such being alone and staring at four walls all day) leads to bad behaviour and it's why some Doodles end up in rescue centres, through no fault of their own. On the other hand, a Labradoodle at the heart

of the family getting plenty of daily exercise is a happy Doodle and a wonderful companion.

Exercising Puppies

We are often asked how much to exercise a pup. It does, of course, vary depending on whether you have a Miniature, Medium or Standard Labradoodle and the dog's natural energy level. Doodle puppies, like babies, have different temperaments and some will be livelier and need more exercise than others.

All puppies require much less exercise than fully-grown dogs. If you over-exercise a growing puppy you can overtire him and damage his developing joints, especially with Standards, causing early arthritis or other issues. The golden rule is to start slowly and build it up. The worst danger is a combination of over exercise and overweight when the puppy is growing.

Do not take him out of the yard or garden until he has completed his vaccinations and it is safe to do so. Then start with short walks on the lead every day. A good guideline is **five minutes exercise per month of age** (up to twice a day) until the puppy is fully grown. That means a total of 15 minutes when he is three months (13 weeks old), 20 minutes when four months (17 weeks) old, and so on.

Slowly increase the time as he gets used to being exercised and this will gradually build up his muscles and stamina. Once he is fully grown, he can go out for much longer. Puppies have enquiring minds. They should

be allowed out for exercise every day in a safe and secure area, such an enclosed garden or yard, or they may become frustrated and develop bad habits.

This, however, is no substitute for exploring new environments and socialising with other dogs and people. Get your pup used to being outside the home environment and experiencing new situations as soon as he is clear after vaccinations.

Under no circumstances leave a puppy imprisoned in a crate for hours on end. Labradoodles, more than most dogs, are extremely sociable and they do not like being left alone for long periods. They often do better with other Labradoodles, but remember that each Labradoodle doubles your costs.

If you are considering getting two puppies, it is a good idea to wait until the first pup has grown into an adult, so he can teach the new arrival some good manners. Another point to consider is that if you keep two puppies from the same litter, their first loyalty may be the one with them since birth – i.e. their loyalty to each other, rather than to you as their owner. They may also be harder to train.

Start to train your puppy to come back to you so that you are soon confident enough to let him roam off the leash. See **Chapter 6. Training** for more information. By the time he's one-year-old you can start to build up to proper walks. Although, these days, many Standard Labradoodles are growing into very large dogs and they can take up to 18 months to finish growing.

Remember, a long, healthy life is best started slowly.

As already outlined, your Labradoodle will get used to an exercise routine. If you over-stimulate and constantly exercise him as a puppy, he will think this is the norm. This is fine with your adorable, playful little pup, but may not be such an attractive prospect when your fully-grown 70lb Labradoodle is demanding constant attention and exercise a year later, or your work patterns change and you have not so much time to devote to him. The key is to start a routine you can stick to.

When, a couple of years later, your little pup has grown into an adorable adult with a skeleton capable of carrying him through a long and healthy life, it will have been worth all the effort and care in the beginning.

Socialisation

Your adult Labradoodle's character will depend largely on two things. The first is his temperament, which he is born with and presumably one of the reasons you have chosen a Labradoodle. Again, the importance of picking a reputable breeder who selects breeding stock based on a good temperament as well as physical characteristics cannot be over-emphasized.

The second factor is environment – or how you bring him up and treat him. In other words, it's a combination of nature and nurture. One essential aspect of nurture is socialisation. Even though Labradoodles are non-aggressive, sociable dogs, you must spend time introducing them to other dogs and humans, as well as noises and traffic, from an early age.

The ultimate goal of socialisation is to have a happy, well-adjusted dog that you can take anywhere. Socialisation will give your dog confidence and teach him not to be afraid of new experiences. Mixing with other dogs and people in different environments, experiencing different sights and sounds will help him to adjust to the human and canine world around him. Timidity, boisterousness, excessive barking, jumping up at people, over-protection and aggression are all signs of poor training and socialisation.

Although Labradoodles are not aggressive dogs by nature, aggression is often grounded in fear, and a dog which mixes easily is less likely to be aggressive. Without frequent and new experiences, some dogs can become timid and nervous when introduced to new experiences.

Fortunately, Labradoodles are inquisitive and love new experiences, provided they are introduced in the right way. As soon as your puppy has had all his jabs and got the all-clear to go out, start introducing him to other dogs in the neighbourhood.

However nervous you are about introducing your adorable little Doodle pup to bigger dogs, it has to be done!

Just make sure that the conditions are right so that your pup will not be intimidated by the whole experience. Try and get together with a friend or friends with non-aggressive dogs on neutral territory in the beginning so that neither dog feels he has to protect his patch. Puppy classes are another great way of getting him used to other dogs while learning discipline.

As with humans, getting out to different places and mixing is both sociable and healthy. Dogs are pack animals. If properly socialised they enjoy meeting or playing with other dogs.

Take your new dog everywhere you can. You want him to feel relaxed and calm in any situation, even noisy and crowded ones. Take treats with you and praise him when he reacts calmly to new situations.

Once he has settled in to your home, introduce him to your friends and teach him not to jump up. If you have young children, it is not only the dog who needs socialising! Youngsters also need training on how to act around dogs, so both parties learn to respect the other.

Exercise Tips

* Never exercise your dog on a full stomach as this can cause bloat,

particularly in large dogs. Your dog should not be given rigorous exercise within an hour before or after eating.

Canine bloat happens when something goes wrong during food digestion. It causes gases to build up quickly in the stomach, blowing up the stomach like a balloon. This cuts off normal blood circulation to and from the heart.

The dog can go into shock and then cardiac arrest within hours of the start of bloat. If you suspect this is happening, get him to a vet immediately. Larger breeds like the Standard Labradoodle are more susceptible than smaller breeds. See our **Chapter 9. Health** for more information.

* Do not throw a ball or toy repeatedly for a puppy, as he may run and run to fetch it in order to please you - or because he thinks it is a great game. He may become over-tired, damage his joints, pull a muscle, strain his heart or otherwise damage himself.

* The same goes for swimming, which most Labradoodles love. Swimming is an exhausting exercise for a dog, and while it is great fun for him to fetch a ball or stick, stop the activity after a while, no matter how much he begs you. Repeatedly retrieving from water may cause him to overstretch himself and get into difficulties. When a dog is over-

exercised, it can place a strain on his heart – just like with humans.

* If you want your Labradoodle to fetch a ball, don't fetch it back yourself or he will never learn to retrieve! The best way is to train him to retrieve while young by giving him praise or a treat when he brings the ball or toy back to your feet.

* Many Labradoodles love snow. If you live in an area with a lot of the white stuff, you may want to invest in a set of doggie boots for the winter. Many Labradoodles have the type of fur on their legs which attracts sticky snow. This results in their paws and legs becoming covered in snowballs, which can actually be quite painful for your dog. Some owners bathe their dog's legs in lukewarm water when they come home covered in snowballs. **Never** bathe them in hot water.

* Some dogs have a stubborn streak, particularly adolescent ones who are pushing the boundaries. If your Labradoodle stares at you and tries to pull or lead you in another direction, ignore him. Do not return his stare as he is challenging you. Just continue along the way YOU want to go, not him!

* Try and vary your exercise route – it will be more interesting for you and the dog.

* Make sure your dog has constant access to fresh water. Dogs can't

sweat and some Labradoodles don't shed hair either. They need to drink water to cool down.

Admittedly, on those horrendous days when it is pouring down with rain, freezing cold (or scorching hot in some places), the last thing you want to do is to venture outdoors with your dog.

But, the lows are more than compensated for by the highs. Daily exercise helps you to bond with your dog, it helps keep you and your Labradoodle fit and healthy, you'll experience new scenery and socialise with other companions – both canine and human.

Trust me, it will enhance both your lives.

9. Labradoodle Health

The best piece of advice for anybody looking to get a healthy Labradoodle is: **buy a well-bred puppy**.

Scientists have come to realise the important role that genetics play in determining a person's long-term health. Well, the same is true of dogs. This means ensuring you get your puppy from a reputable breeder who selects the parent dogs based on a number of factors.

It doesn't matter whether the dam and sire are pedigree (purebred) Poodles and Labradors or F1, F2, F3 or multigeneration Labradoodle crosses, a good Labradoodle breeder selects their breeding stock based on:

- **bloodline**
- **health history**
- **temperament**
- **coat**
- **conformation**
- **body shape**

Far better to spend time choosing a dog which has been properly bred than to spend a lot of time and money later at the vet's after he develops health or behaviour problems due to poor breeding.

Another advantage of choosing a good, experienced breeder is that you have a better idea of what your Doodle will look like and how big he or she will grow. Many first-time owners are surprised when a year or so down the line, their fluffy little Labradoodle pup stand as tall as the kitchen table!

As the English upper classes say (in a very posh accent): *"There is no substitute for good breeding, darling!"* So spend some time on research into finding a reputable breeder. Follow these links for details of accredited breeders in different countries:

UK: www.labradoodle.org.uk/findbreeder.php
USA: http://ilainc.net/guest/MemberBreederList.aspx
    www.australianlabradoodleclub.us/information_links/Breeder-Members.htm
Australia: www.laa.org.au/ala-breeder/Australia.htm

Robust Labradoodles

Labradoodles are crossbreeds and generally pretty robust. They are relatively free of many genetic problems that affect some other breeds. But like any pure breed or crossbreed, the Labradoodle is susceptible to certain inherited diseases.

Diseases within purebreds are often widespread, so putting two dogs together from different breeds doesn't necessarily mean that a healthier pup will emerge. For a more detailed discussion, read our section on **Hybrid Vigour**. According to Veterinary Pet Insurance: "The Labradoodle's health history is still being determined, but thus far has shown health concerns similar to those of Labradors and Poodles."

This means that a Labradoodle may inherit diseases from the Labrador and/or the Poodle. Careful breeding will minimise the risk, so selecting the right breeder is extremely important. As with any pet, you will probably encounter some health issues during the hopefully many years of your dog's life. Advances in veterinary medicine have meant that many diseases which were once fatal can now be successfully treated, but often the key to good outcomes is early diagnosis and treatment.

Disclaimer: *We are not canine health experts. If you are worried about your Labradoodle's health, our advice is always the same: consult a veterinarian.*

Firstly, how can you tell if your dog is in good health? Well, our **Top Ten Signs** are a good start. Here are some positive things to look for in a healthy Labradoodle:

Top 10 Signs of a Healthy Dog

1. **Eyes** - a healthy dog's eyes are shiny and bright. The area around the eyeball (the conjunctiva) should be a healthy pink. Paleness could be a sign of underlying problems. There should be no thick, green or yellow discharge from the eyes. A cloudy eye may be a sign of cataracts.

2. **Coats** - these are easy-to-monitor indicators of a healthy dog. They should be full and pleasant to the touch. Many Labradoodles have fleecy or wiry

coats and these should be springy and full of life. Labradoodles with fur more akin to the Labrador should have a smoother, shiny coat. A dull, lifeless coat can be a sign that something is amiss.

3. **Skin** - This should be smooth without redness. (Normal skin pigment can vary from light to pink, black, brown or even blue according to the colour of the Labradoodle.) Open sores, scales, scabs or growths can be a sign of a problem. Signs of fleas, ticks and other external parasites should be treated immediately.

4. **Ears** – ear infections can be a particular problem with Labradoodles and other breeds which do not shed a lot, such as Schnauzers. Your dog's ears should be clean with no dark or bloody discharge. Redness or swelling can be a sign of problems.
If you have a Labradoodle who does not shed, or who hardly sheds, you should check his ears regularly and hand-pluck hairs from inside the ear if necessary. This does not hurt the dog and, once used to it, can become a normal part of regular grooming. Offer your dog a treat at the end of ear-plucking. You, like us, can also ask your groomer to pluck any excess ear hair each visit to stop the ears becoming clogged with hair.

The warm place under the ear flap is an ideal breeding ground for mites and infections, especially with miniature Labradoodles who have narrower ear canals. The ears should smell normal and not be hot. A bad smell, a hot ear or one full of brown wax is often a sign of infection, so get him to the vet or it could ultimately lead to a burst eardrum or even deafness.

5. **Mouth** – Gums should be pink or pigmented with black. Paleness can be a sign of anaemia. Red, inflamed gums can be a sign of gingivitis or other tooth disease. Again, your Labradoodle's breath should smell OK. Young dogs will have sparkling white teeth, whereas older dogs will have darker teeth, but they should not have any hard white, yellow, green or brown bits.

6. **Weight** – your Labradoodle should be the correct weight and have a healthy appetite. The rib, back and hip bones should not show, but you should be able to feel them under the skin. Dogs may have weight problems due to factors such as diet, allergies, diabetes, thyroid or other problems. A general rule of thumb is that your Labradoodle's stomach should be in a line or above his rib cage when standing. If his stomach hangs below, he is overweight or he may have a pot belly which can be a sign that something is amiss, such as Cushing's Disease.

7. **Nose** - a dog's nose is an indicator of health symptoms. It could be black, pink or mottled. But whatever colour, it should normally be moist and cold to the touch. The moistness should be free from clear, watery secretions. Any yellow, green or foul smelling discharge is not normal. In younger dogs this can be a sign of canine distemper.

8. **Temperature** - The normal temperature of a dog is 101°F. Excited or exercising dogs may run a slightly higher temperature. Anything above 103°F or below 100°F should be checked out. The exceptions are female dogs that are about to give birth who will often have a temperature of 99°F. If you take your dog's temperature, make sure he is relaxed first and always use a purpose-made thermometer.

9. **Attitude** - a generally positive attitude and personality is the sign of good health. Symptoms of illness may be lethargy, sleeping a lot, not eating food or a general lack of interest in surroundings.

10. **Energy** – Generally, Labradoodles are regarded as dogs with medium energy levels, although many may be more active. Your dog should have good energy levels with fluid and pain-free movements. Lethargy or lack of energy - if it is not the dog's normal character - could be a sign of an underlying problem.

So now you know some of the signs of a healthy dog – what are the signs of an unhealthy one? There are many different symptoms that can indicate your beloved canine companion isn't feeling great. If you don't know your dog, then we recommend you spend some time getting to do so.

What are his normal character and temperament? Lively or sedate, playful or serious, happy to be alone or loves to be with people, a keen appetite or a fussy eater? How often does he empty his bowels, does he ever vomit? (Dogs will often eat grass to make themselves sick, this is perfectly normal and a canine's natural way of cleansing their digestive system.)

You may think your Labradoodle can't talk, **but he can!** If you really know your dog, his character and habits, then he CAN tell you when he's not well. He does this by changing his patterns. Some symptoms are physical, some emotional and others are behavioural. It's important for you to be able to recognise these changes as soon as possible. Early treatment can be the key to keeping a simple problem from snowballing into a serious illness.

If you think your Labradoodle is unwell, it is useful to keep an accurate and detailed account of his symptoms to give to the vet. This will help him or her correctly diagnose and effectively treat your dog. Most canine illnesses are detected through a combination of signs and symptoms. Here are some signs that your dog may be unwell:

Four Vital Signs of Illness

1. Temperature
A newborn puppy will have a temperature of 94-97º F. This will reach the normal adult body temperature of 101ºF at about four weeks old. Anything between 100ºF and 102ºF is normal.

Like all dogs, a Labradoodle's temperature is normally taken via his rectum. Be very careful when doing this – especially with lively Doodles. It's easier to get someone to hold your dog while you do this. Digital thermometers are a good choice, but **only use one specifically made for rectal use,** as normal glass thermometers can easily break off in the rectum. Ear thermometers are now available, making the task much easier, although they can be expensive and don't suit all dogs' ears.

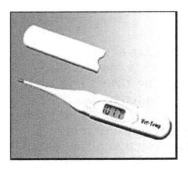

Remember - exercise or excitement can cause the temperature to rise by 2ºF - 3ºF when the dog is actually in good health. If your dog's temperature is above or below the norms, get him to the vet.

2. Respiratory Rate
Another symptom of canine illness is a change in breathing patterns. This varies a lot depending on the size and weight of the dog. An adult dog will have a respiratory rate of 15-25 breaths per minute when resting. You can easily check this by counting your dog's breaths for a minute with a stopwatch handy. Don't do this if the dog is panting - it doesn't count.

3. Heart Rate
You can feel for your dog's heartbeat by placing your hand on his lower ribcage - just behind the elbow. Don't be alarmed if the heartbeat seems

irregular compared to a human. It IS irregular in many dogs. Have your vet show you how and get used to your dog's normal heartbeat.

* Big dogs like Standard Labradoodles have a normal rate of 70 to 120 beats per minute.
* Medium Labradoodles have a normal rate of 80 to 120 beats per minute.
* Small dogs like Miniature Labradoodles have a normal rate of 90 to 140 beats per minute.

4. Behaviour Changes

Classic symptoms of illness are any inexplicable behaviour changes.
If there has NOT been a change in the household atmosphere, such as another new pet, a new baby, moving home or the absence of a family member, then the following symptoms may well be a sign that all is not well with your Labradoodle:

- Depression
- Anxiety
- Tiredness
- Trembling
- Falling or stumbling
- Loss of appetite
- Walking in circles

If your dog shows any of these signs, he needs to be kept under close watch for a few hours or even days. Quite often he will return to normal of his own accord. Like humans, dogs have off-days too. If he is showing any of the above symptoms, then don't over-exercise him and try to avoid stressful situations. Make sure he has access to clean water. There are many other signals of ill health, but these are four of the most important.

Keep a record for your vet. If your dog does need professional medical attention, most vets will want to know -
WHEN the symptoms first appeared
WHETHER they are getting better or worse, and
HOW FREQUENT the symptoms are. Are they intermittent, continuous or increasing in frequency?

We have listed some canine maladies which may affect Labradoodles and, importantly, the signs to look out for. It is by no means a complete list and if you are at all worried about your dog's health, make an appointment to see a vet. Out next chapter is devoted to Labradoodle Skin.

PRA (Progressive Retinal Atrophy)

PRA is the name for several progressive diseases which lead to blindness. First recognized at the beginning of the 20th century in Gordon Setters, this inherited condition has been documented in over 100 breeds and some mixed breeds.

Labradors, Labradoodles, Australian Labradoodles, Golden Retrievers and Goldendoodles are all recognised are being among the breeds and crossbreeds which may be affected by the disease.

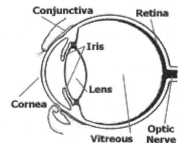

The specific genetic disorder which may affect Labradoodles is called prcd-PRA (progressive rod-cone degeneration PRA.)

 It causes cells in the retina at the back of the eye to degenerate and die, even though the cells seem to develop normally early in life. The 'rod' cells operate in low light levels and are the first to lose normal function. Night blindness results.

Then the 'cone' cells gradually lose their normal function in full light situations. Most affected dogs will eventually go blind. Typically, the disease is recognised first in early adolescence or early adulthood. Conditions that might look like prcd-PRA could be another disease and might not be inherited.

It's important to remember that not all retinal disease is PRA and not all PRA is the prcd form of PRA. Annual eye exams by a veterinary ophthalmologist will build a history of eye health that will help to diagnose disease.

Prcd-PRA is inherited as a recessive trait. This means that the faulty gene must be inherited **from each parent** in order to cause disease in an offspring. In other words, each parent was either a carrier or sufferer. It's been proven that all breeds tested for *prcd*-PRA have the same mutated gene, even though the disease may develop at different ages or severities from one breed to another.

Sadly, there is no cure, but prcd-PRA can be avoided in future generations by testing dogs before breeding. If your dog is affected it may be helpful to read other owners' experiences living with blind dogs at www.eyevet.org and www.blinddogs.com.

Eye Testing
There are various ways of testing for hereditary eye conditions. In the USA there is the OptiGen prcd-PRA Test and the Canine Eye Registration Foundation (CERF).

In the UK there is the British Veterinary Association (BVA) Eye Test, an annual test, carried out due to the fact some diseases have a late onset. If you are buying a puppy, it is highly advisable to check if the parents have been tested and given the all-clear. Always ensure the breeder lets you see the original certificate (which is white in the UK) and not a photocopy. Identification of dogs that do not carry diseased genes is the key to eradicating the problem.

Hereditary Cataracts

These can be found in Labradors, Golden Retrievers, Standard Poodles and certain other breeds. Inheritance of hereditary cataracts varies between breeds with some showing recessive inheritance and others dominant. It is therefore very important that both parents of the Labradoodle puppy for sale have a clear current annual eye certificate.

Healthy Canine Eye

Research has shown that Labradors and Golden Retrievers can be diagnosed with hereditary cataracts at any time up to old age and the clear annual eye tests discussed above are essential for a breeding dog. The severity of the cataracts in Retrievers varies considerably, while in Standard Poodles hereditary cataracts usually only appear in young dogs, but it is equal in both eyes and causes blindness.

Diagnosis

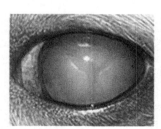 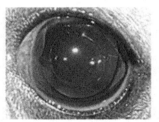

Left: eye with cataracts. Right: same eye with artificial lens

Hereditary cataracts are usually first diagnosed when the owner sees their dog bumping into furniture, or when his pupils have changed colour. The vet will refer the pet to the specialist who will carry out the same eye exam that is done for breeding stock.

The process is painless and simple, drops are put into the eyes and after a few minutes the dog is taken into a dark room for examination and diagnosis. Corrective surgery is possible, but the patient must be suitable for a quiet post-operative period.

The annual eye test carried out by an eye specialist looks for the early signs of this disease so that affected dogs are not bred to pass on his condition to their puppies. All good Labradoodle breeders eye test and will show you the current certificate for the mother and a copy of the father's if he is elsewhere.

Treatment

If you think your Labradoodle may have cataracts, it's important to get him to a vet ASAP. Early removal of cataracts can restore vision and provide a dramatic improvement in the quality of your dog's life.

The only treatment for canine cataracts is surgery (unless the cataracts are caused by another condition like canine diabetes). Despite what you may have heard, laser surgery does not exist for canine cataracts, neither is there any proven medical treatment other than surgery.

The good news is that surgery is almost always (85-90%) successful. The dog has to have a general anaesthetic but the operation is often performed on an outpatient basis. The procedure is similar to small incision cataract surgery in people. An artificial lens is often implanted in the dog's eye to replace the cataract lens. Dogs can see without an artificial lens, but the image will not be in focus. Discuss with the vet or ophthalmologist whether your dog would benefit from an artificial lens.

Even better news is that once the cataract is removed, it does not recur. However before your dog can undergo this procedure, he has to be fit and healthy and a suitable candidate for surgery.

After the operation, he will probably have to stay at the surgery overnight so that the professionals can keep an eye on him. Once back home, he will have to wear a protective Elizabethan collar, or E collar, for about one to two weeks while his eye is healing.

You have to keep him quiet and calm (not always easy with Labradoodles!) You'll also have to give him eye drops, perhaps four times a day for the first week and then less frequently after that. The success of cataract surgery depends very much on the owner doing all the right things. But all the effort will be worth it when your Labradoodle regains his sight.

Hip Dysplasia

Canine Hip Dysplasia (CHD) is the most common cause of hind leg lameness in dogs. It is a hereditary condition which occurs mainly in large, fast-growing dogs such as Standard Labradoodles.

Several factors contribute to the development of the disease and some breeds are genetically predisposed to the disease, including Labradors, Golden Retrievers, German Shepherds, Rottweilers and Giant Schnauzers. Smaller breeds may also suffer, but the effects are not as obvious.

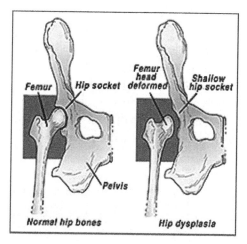

The hip is a ball and socket joint. Hip dysplasia is caused when the head of the femur (thigh bone) fits loosely into a shallow and poorly-developed socket in the pelvis. The right hand side of our picture shows a shallow hip socket and a deformed femur head, causing hip dysplasia. The healthy joint is on the left.

Most dogs with dysplasia are born with normal hips but due to their genetic make-up - and possibly other factors such as diet - the soft tissues that surround the joint develop abnormally.

The joint carrying the weight of the dog and becomes loose and unstable, muscle growth lags behind normal development and is often followed by degenerative joint disease or osteoarthritis, which is the body's attempt to stabilize the loose hip joint. Early diagnosis gives your vet the best chance to tackle the problem as soon as possible, minimising the chance of arthritis developing. Symptoms range from mild discomfort to extreme pain. A puppy with canine hip dysplasia usually starts to show signs between five and 13 months old.

Symptoms

- *Lameness in hind legs, particularly after exercise*
- *Difficulty or stiffness when getting up or climbing uphill*
- *A 'bunny hop' gait*
- *Dragging the rear end when getting up*
- *Waddling rear leg gait*
- *A painful reaction to stretching the hind legs, resulting in a short stride*
- *A side-to-side sway of the croup (area above the tail) with a tendency to tilt the hips down if you push down on the croup*

- *A reluctance to jump, exercise or climb stairs*

Causes and Triggers

Canine hip dysplasia is usually an inherited condition. But there are also factors which can trigger or worsen the condition, including:

1. Overfeeding, especially on a diet high in protein and calories
2. Excess calcium, also usually due to overfeeding
3. Extended periods without exercise – or too much vigorous exercise - especially when your dog's bones are growing
4. Obesity

Advances in nutritional research have shown that diet plays an important role in the development of hip dysplasia.

Feeding a high-calorie diet to growing dogs can trigger a predisposition to hip dysplasia, as the rapid weight gain places increased stress on the hips. During their first year of life, Standard Labradoodle puppies should be fed a special large breed growth diet which will contain the correct amount of calories, minerals and protein, thereby reducing the risk of hip dysplasia. When you take your puppy to the vet's for his injections, ask for advice on the best diet.

Exercise may be another risk factor. Dogs that have a predisposition to the disease may have an increased chance of getting it if they are over-exercised at a young age. On the other hand, dogs with large leg muscle mass are **less** likely to get dysplasia than dogs with small muscle mass. The key here is moderate, low impact exercise for fast-growing young dogs. Activities which  strengthen the gluteus muscles, such as running and swimming, are probably a good idea. Whereas high impact activity that apply a lot of force to the joint, such and jumping and catching Frisbees, is not recommended with big young Labradoodles.

Treatment

As with most conditions, early detection leads to a better outcome. Your vet will take X-rays to make a diagnosis. Treatment is geared towards preventing the hip joint getting worse and decreasing pain. Various medical and surgical treatments are now available to ease the dog's discomfort and restore some mobility.

Treatment depends upon several factors, such as the dog's age, how bad the problem is and, sadly, how much money you can afford to spend on treatment.

Management of the condition usually consists of restricting exercise, keeping body weight down and then managing pain with analgesics and anti-inflammatory drugs.

As with humans, cortisone injections may sometimes be used to reduce inflammation and swelling. Cortisone can be injected directly into the affected hip to provide almost immediate relief for a tender, swollen joint. In severe cases, surgery may be an option, especially with older dogs.

Hip Testing

Both the dam and sire of your puppy should have been 'hip scored' - or tested - for hip dysplasia and the results available for you to see. Thirty years ago the British Veterinary Association and Kennel Club set up a hip screening programme for dogs, which tests them using radiology and gives them a rating or 'hip score'.

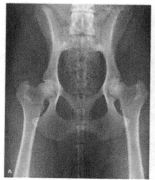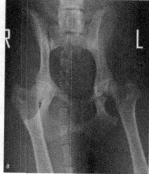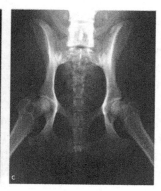

Figure A is the healthy hip, B shows lateral tilting, C shows outward rotation

The Breed Mean Score (BMS) for Labradoodles is 13 and the Median is 11. Responsible breeders should only breed from stock which has a hip score well below 13, ideally below 11. The Kennel Club is responsible for publishing hip dysplasia results for all pedigree dogs in the Kennel Club Breed Records. However, as the Labradoodle is a cross breed, the KC does not hold the information.

The current cost of a hip score is only £55, the cost of a joint hip and elbow test is £100. With the price of a Labradoodle puppy running to many hundreds or even thousands of pounds (or dollars), all breeders can afford to have their potential breeding stock tested.

Ethically, they **should** have all stock tested, as non-breeding from dogs carrying the hip dysplasia genes is the way to reduce this painful disease.

When buying a Labradoodle pup, ask to see the original hip score certificate, which is green in the UK. If the breeder does not own the stud dog, a photocopy of his results should also be available. The same applies with elbow tests outlined below, when results are on a gold-coloured form.

Veterinary MRI and radiology specialist Ruth Dennis, of the Animal Health Trust, states: *"For dogs intended for breeding, it is essential that the hips are assessed before mating to ensure that they are free of dysplastic changes or only minimally affected."*

To recap: If you are getting a Labradoodle puppy, particularly a Standard, ask if there is any history of hip, elbow or eye problems in either of the parents and ask to see their test certificates.

Elbow Dysplasia

Elbow dysplasia is more commonly seen in fast-growing large puppies and is not a simple condition to understand nor easy to explain. It is really a syndrome in which one or more conditions are present.

The exact cause is unknown, but it is probably due to a combination of genetic factors, over-nutrition with rapid growth, trauma and hormonal factors. Affected dogs include Labradors, Golden Retrievers, Rottweilers, Bernese Mountain Dogs, Newfoundlands, German Shepherds and Chow Chows. Signs usually begin between four to 12 months of age.

Many bones in a newborn puppy are not a single piece of bone, but several different pieces with cartilage in between. This is especially true of long limb bones.

As the puppy grows, the cartilage changes into bone and several pieces of bone fuse together forming one entire bone. For instance, the ulna, a bone in the forearm, starts out as four pieces that eventually fuse into one bone.

Elbow dysplasia occurs when certain parts of the joint develop abnormally as a dog grows. Some parts of the joint may have abnormal development, resulting in an uneven joint surface, inflammation, lameness and arthritis. It eventually results in elbow arthritis which may be associated with joint stiffness (reduced range of motion) and lameness.

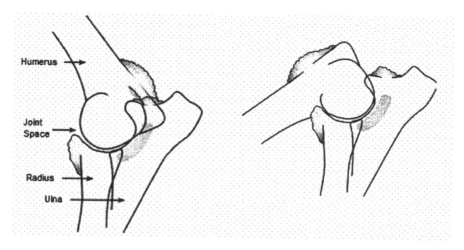

Figure 4a   Figure 4b

Figures 4a and 4b. Osteoarthritic changes to the shape and structure of the elbow joint. The shaded areas on figure 4a (extended elbow) and 4b (flexed elbow) represent the changes to bone and cartilage as a result of UAP and other forms of elbow dysplasia.
Images courtesy of the British Veterinary Association.

Symptoms

The most notable symptom is a limp. Your Labradoodle may hold his leg out away from his body while walking, or even lift a front leg completely, putting no weight on it. Signs may be noted as early as four months old and many dogs will go through a period between six months and a year old when symptoms will be at their worst. After this, most will occasionally show some less severe signs.
As the adolescent matures, there will probably be permanent arthritic changes.

Diagnosis

Many dogs will have more than one of the conditions that contribute to elbow dysplasia. One or both elbows may be affected. The symptoms of front leg lameness and pain in the elbow are typical. However, there are other conditions that can affect the front leg of a young dog that closely mimic the signs of elbow dysplasia. Your vet will take X-rays of the affected joint or joints for a proper diagnosis.

Treatment

Treatment varies depending on the exact cause of the condition. The young dog is usually placed on a regular, low-impact exercise programme - swimming can be a good exercise. Owners must carefully manage their dog's diet and weight. Oral or injected medication such as nonsteroidal anti-inflammatory drugs (NSAIDS) may be necessary to make him more comfortable, prescribed to reduce pain and inflammation.

After the age of 12 to 18 months, the dog's lameness becomes less severe and some function very well. Elbow dysplasia is a lifelong problem, although some can be very effectively helped with surgery. In most cases, degenerative joint disease (arthritis) will occur as the dog gets older, regardless of the type of treatment.

Luxating Patella

Luxating patella, also called *'floating kneecap'* or *'slipped stifle'* is a painful condition akin to a dislocated knee cap. It is often congenital (present from birth) and more typically affects toy and small breeds, including Miniature and Toy Poodles. However Labradors are also particularly prone to luxating patella - they are the fifth worse breed for it - which means that both small and large Labradoodles can be affected.

Symptoms
A typical sign would be if your dog is running across the park when he suddenly pulls up short and yelps with pain. He might limp on three legs and then after a period of about 10 minutes, drop the affected leg and start to walk normally again.

If the condition is severe, he may hold up the affected leg up for a few days. Dogs who have a luxating patella on both hind legs may change their gait completely, dropping their hindquarters and holding the rear legs further out from the body as they walk. In the most extreme cases they might not even use their rear legs, but walk like a circus act by balancing on their front legs so their hindquarters don't touch the ground.

Typically most sufferers are middle-aged dogs with a history of intermittent lameness in the affected rear leg or legs.

Causes
A groove in the end of the femur (thigh bone) allows the knee cap to glide up and down when the knee joint is bent, while keeping it in place at the same time. If this groove is too shallow, the knee cap may luxate – or dislocate. It can only return to its natural position when the quadriceps muscle relaxes and increases in length, which is why the dog may have to hold his leg up for some time after the dislocation.

Treatment
If left untreated, the groove will become even shallower and the dog will become progressively lamer, with arthritis prematurely affecting the joint. This will cause a permanently swollen knee and reduce your Labradoodle's mobility.

It is therefore important if you suspect your dog may have a luxating patella to get him in for a check-up by your vet as soon as possible.

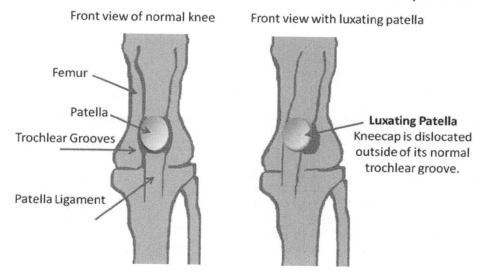

Front view of normal knee   Front view with luxating patella

Femur

Patella

Trochlear Grooves

Luxating Patella
Kneecap is dislocated outside of its normal trochlear groove.

Patella Ligament

One option is surgery. The groove at the base of the femur may be surgically deepened to better hold the knee cap in place. This operation is known as a '*trochlear modification*'. There are ways of tackling the problem with different forms of surgery. The good news is that dogs generally respond well, whatever the type of surgery, and are usually completely recovered within one to two months.

von Willebrand's Disease

Von Willebrand's Disease is a common inherited bleeding disorder similar to haemophilia in humans. In Von Willebrand's Disease (vWD), the dog lacks a substance which helps to form blood clots.

Technically speaking this substance (called 'von Willebrand's factor') forms clots and stabilises something called Factor VIII in the normal clotting process. Dogs with von Willebrand's Disease bleed excessively as their blood does not clot properly. Some breeds have a higher incidence of vWD than others, including Standard Poodles and Golden Retrievers.

Humans can also suffer from vWD. This disease is named after Erik Adolf von Willebrand, a Finnish doctor who documented and studied a rare bleeding disorder in an isolated group of people in 1924. He showed that the disease was inherited, rather than caught by infection.

Symptoms

The main symptom is excessive bleeding, which usually occurs after an injury or surgery. In these cases the blood simply does not clot in the normal time and bleeding is profuse. Dogs with Von Willebrand's disease can also develop nosebleeds or bleeding from the gums.

Bleeding can also occur in the stomach or intestine. If this is the case, you may notice something unusual in your dog's faeces; his stools may have blood in them or be black and tarry. Some dogs will have blood in their urine, while others may have bleeding in their joints. In this last case, the symptoms are similar to those of arthritis.

Diagnosis

The diagnosis is made through a test to check the levels of von Willebrand's factor in the blood. If you are buying a puppy, you can check that the parents have been DNA tested for vWD and ask to see the certificate giving them the all-clear.

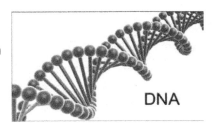

DNA

Treatment

Sadly, as yet there is no cure for von Willebrand's Disease. The only way to stop the spread of the disease is to have dogs tested and to prevent breeding from affected animals. Without treatment, a dog can bleed to death after surgery or what otherwise might normally be considered a less than life-threatening injury. The only proven way to treat vWD is with transfusions of blood collected from healthy dogs.

Some dogs with Von Willebrand's Disease also are hypothyroid, meaning they have lower than normal levels of thyroid hormone. These dogs benefit from thyroid hormone replacement therapy. A drug called DDAVP may help dogs with bleeding episodes. It can be administered into the nose to increase clotting, but opinion is still divided as to whether this treatment is effective.

Hypothyroidism

Hypothyroidism is a common hormonal disorder in dogs and is due to an under-active thyroid gland. The gland (located on either side of the windpipe in the dog's throat) does not produce enough of the hormone thyroid, which controls the speed of the metabolism. Dogs with very low thyroid levels have a slow metabolic rate. It occurs mainly in dogs over the age of five. Standard Labradoodles may be more prone to hypothyroidism than some other breeds.

Generally, hypothyroidism occurs most frequently in large, middle-aged dogs of either gender. The symptoms are often non-specific and quite gradual in onset, and they may vary depending on breed and age. Most forms of hypothyroidism are diagnosed with a blood test.

Common Symptoms

The following symptoms have been listed in order, with the most common ones being at the top of the list:

*High blood cholesterol
*Lethargy
*Hair Loss
*Weight gain or obesity
*Dry coat or excessive shedding
*Hyper pigmentation or darkening of the skin, seen in 25% of cases
*Intolerance to cold, seen in 15% of dogs with the condition

Treatment

Although hypothyroidism is a type of auto-immune disease and cannot be prevented, symptoms can usually be easily diagnosed and treated. Most affected dogs can be well-managed on thyroid hormone replacement therapy tablets. The dog is placed on a daily dose of a synthetic thyroid hormone called thyroxine (levothyroxine).

The patient is usually given a standard dose for his weight and then blood samples are taken periodically to check his response and the dose is adjusted accordingly. Depending upon your dog's preferences and needs, the medication can be given in different forms, such as a solid tablet, in liquid form, or a gel that can be rubbed into your Labradoodle's ears.

Once treatment has started, he will be on it for the rest of his life.

In some less common situations, surgery may be required to remove part or all of the thyroid gland. Another treatment is radioiodine, where radioactive iodine is used to kill the overactive cells of the thyroid. While this is considered one of the most effective treatments, not all animals are suitable for the procedure and lengthy hospitalisation is often required. Happily, once the diagnosis has been made and treatment has started, whichever treatment your dog undergoes, the majority of symptoms disappear.

NOTE: **Hyper**thyroidism (as opposed to **hypo**thyroidism) is caused by the thyroid gland producing **too much** thyroid hormone. It's quite rare in dogs, more often seen in cats. A common symptom
is the dog being ravenously hungry, but losing weight.

Canine Bloat

Canine bloat is a serious medical condition which requires urgent medical attention. Without it, the dog can die. Bloat is known by several different names: twisted stomach, gastric torsion or, to give the ailment its medical term, Gastric Dilitation-Volvulus (GDV). It occurs when the dog's body becomes overstretched with too much gas.

The reasons for it are not fully understood, but there are some well-known risk factors. Bloat occurs mainly in larger breeds, particularly those with deep chests like Great Danes, Doberman Pinschers and Setters, but these are not the only breeds affected and it can happen to smaller dogs.

It also happens more - but not exclusively- to dogs over seven years of age and it is more common in males than in females. The risks increase if the stomach is very full, either with food or with water. A dog which is fed once daily and eats very quickly, or gets access to the food store and gorges itself, could be at higher risk. Exercising after eating or after a big drink also increases the risk, and stress can also act as a trigger.

Bloat occurs when gas is taken in as the dog eats or drinks. It can occur with or without the stomach twisting (volvulus). As the stomach swells with gas, it can rotate 90° to 360°. The twisting stomach traps air, food, and water inside and the bloated organ stops blood flowing properly to veins in the abdomen, leading to low blood pressure, shock and even damage to internal organs.

Bloat can kill a dog in less than one hour. If you suspect your Labradoodle has bloat, get him into the car and off to the vet immediately. Even with treatment, mortality rates range from 10% to 60%. With surgery, this drops to 15% to 33%.

Causes
Despite research, the causes are not completely clear. However, the following conditions are generally thought to be contributory factors:

* Air is gulped down as the dog eats or drinks. This is thought more likely to cause a problem when the dog's bowls are on the floor. Some owners

buy or construct a frame for the bowls so they are at chest height. However, some experts believe that this may actually increase the risk of bloat. Discuss the situation with your vet. Another option is to moisten your dog's food to slow him down.

* A large meal eaten once a day. For this reason, many owners of large dogs feed their dog two smaller feeds every day.

* Diet may be a factor: avoid dog food with high fats or which use citric acid as a preservative, also avoid food with tiny pieces of kibble. Don't overfeed your dog, try and prevent him from eating too fast and avoid feeding scraps as these may upset his stomach and lead to bloat.

* Drinking too much water just before, during or after eating. Remove the water bowl just before mealtimes, but be sure to return it soon after.

* Vigorous exercise before or after eating. Allow one hour either side of mealtimes before allowing your dog strenuous exercise.

* Age, temperament and breeds: older dogs are more susceptible than younger ones and more males suffer than females. Deep-chested dogs are most at risk and some breeds, such as Doberman Pinschers, Great Danes and Giant Schnauzers, have a hereditary disposition for bloat.

* Stress can possibly be a trigger, with nervous and aggressive dogs being more prone to the illness. Try and maintain a peaceful environment for your dog.

Symptoms
Bloat is extremely painful and the dog will show signs of distress, although it may be difficult to distinguish them from other types of stress. He may stand uncomfortably or seem to be anxious for no apparent reason. Another symptom is dry retching: the dog will often attempt to vomit every five to 30 minutes, but nothing is fetched up, except perhaps foam. Other signs include swelling of the abdomen – this will usually feel firm like a drum – general weakness, difficulty breathing or rapid panting, drooling or excessive drinking. His behaviour will change and he may do some of the following: whine, pace up and down, look for a hiding place or lick the air.

Treatment
Bloat is an emergency condition. Get your dog to a veterinary surgery immediately.

Addison's Disease

Addison's Disease in dogs is also known as *'hypoadrenocorticism'*. There are two bean-shaped organs near the kidneys called adrenal glands. Although they are quite small, they produce two critical hormones: cortisol - a hormone which deals with stress - and aldosterone, which regulates the amount of salt in the body. Both are essential for normal bodily functions.

Glucocorticoids such as cortisol have an effect on sugar, fat and protein metabolism. They are partially responsible for the reaction known as 'fight or flight' response during stressful periods. Mineralocorticoids like aldosterone help regulate the electrolytes sodium and potassium in the body, particularly in stressful situations. When the adrenal glands do not function properly, a metabolism and electrolyte imbalance occurs.

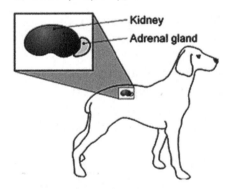

Incidentally, the far more common Cushing's Disease *(hyperadrenocorticism)* is the exact opposite. It occurs when the adrenal gland produces too much of these hormones. Labradoodles are not especially susceptible to Cushing's Disease, however, Standard Poodles are regarded as a high-incidence breed for Addison's Disease, along with German Shepherds, Great Danes, Newfoundlands, West Highland Terriers, Bearded Collies and some other breeds. Golden Retrievers have a particularly low incidence of the disease.

The causes of Addison's Disease are not yet known, although they are generally thought to be genetic, often related to autoimmune disorders. It has symptoms in common with many other ailments, which makes diagnosis difficult and sometimes only arrived at by a process of elimination. But once correctly diagnosed, it can be successfully treated and the dog can live a normal active life.

Symptoms
The symptoms can be vague and may initially simply appear as if the dog is off-colour. Sometimes *hypoglycemia* (low blood sugar) is also present, and Addison's can be initially confused with other problems such as seizure disorders, a pancreatic tumour, food poisoning, twisted stomach, parvovirus, back or joint problems. This has earned Addison's the nicknames 'the Great Mimic' and 'the Great Imitator'.

Symptoms may wax and wane over months or years making diagnosis difficult. If the adrenals continue to deteriorate, ultimately the dog will have an acute episode called an *Addisonian crisis*. At this point many dogs are diagnosed with renal failure, as the kidneys are unable to function properly. Typically they are given IV solutions, which may produce an almost miraculous recovery. This, too, is a great indication that failure of the adrenal glands, rather than of the kidneys, is creating the symptoms.

Addison's more often affects young to middle-aged female dogs; however, a dog of any age and either sex can develop the disease. The average age at diagnosis is four years old, although it has been found in puppies as well as dogs up to 12 years old. Across the general canine population, about 70% of affected dogs are female. But with Standard Poodles, both males and females are susceptible.

Here are some general signs to look out for:

*Lethargy
*Lack of appetite
*Diarrhoea
*Vomiting
 *Weight loss
*Tremors or shaking
*Muscle weakness
*Pain in hindquarters

General muscle weakness might mean that your dog that can't jump onto the bed or sofa as he has done in the past. Shivering or muscle tremors may also be present. The most important thing to remember is that you know your dog better than anyone, so if something seems not right, get it checked out by a vet.

Diagnosis

Diagnosis is confirmed by a blood test called the ACTH stimulation test. However, because the disease is not very common and has a wide variety of symptoms, the test is usually done after several other tests have been carried out to eliminate more common diseases.

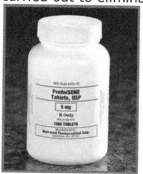

The dog is given an injection of the adrenal-stimulating hormone ACTH. A normal dog will respond by having an increase in blood cortisol. An affected dog will not have this increase and a diagnosis of Addison's Disease is made. Before you reach this stage, one of the first things your vet may test for is electrolyte levels, particularly sodium and potassium. The results may point towards Addison's, but this is not a definitive

155

diagnosis. Other factors, such as whipworms (found in the USA) can also cause irregular electrolyte levels.

Treatment

There are several medications used to treat Addison's. The first type replaces the aldosterone – the hormone responsible for maintaining electrolyte levels. It is replaced with either an oral medication called Florinef (fludrocortisone acetate), which is normally administered twice a day and monitored two or three times a year. A newer, sometimes more effective, option is the injection every 25 days of Percorten-V (DOCP).

In addition, the cortisol, or glucocorticoids, must also be replaced. This is typically done with a low dose of prednisone or hydrocortisone given orally. With atypical and secondary Addison's this is the only medication given.

The dog will need medication and monitoring for the rest of his life, but the good news is that most dogs properly treated for Addison's return to a full and happy life.

Cushing's Disease

Also called '*hyperadrenocorticism*', this is a complex ailment best described as a set of symptoms caused by the dog producing **too much** of a hormone called cortisol. It is the opposite of Addison's Disease, where the adrenal glands are not producing enough hormones. It is a condition that usually develops over a period of time, which is why it is more often seen in older dogs. It affects some Poodles, which means that it may affect some Labradoodles.

Cortisol is released by the adrenal gland located near the kidneys. Normally it is produced during times of stress to prepare the body for strenuous activity. It alters the metabolism, allowing the body to draw energy from stored fats and sugars while retaining sodium and water. Think of an adrenaline rush. The problem occurs when the body is constantly being exposed to cortisol and in effect is in a persistent state of breakdown.

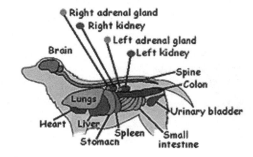

Symptoms

Like Addison's Disease, it can be very difficult to diagnose. The most common signs of Cushing's are similar to those for old age, making it hard to spot and then monitor. If you can, it is a good idea to keep a note of any changes you notice in your dog's habits, behaviour and appearance and take these notes with you to the vet. The disease progresses slowly. Most dogs suffered from at least one symptom of the disease from one to six years before the disease was diagnosed. Some dogs will have only one symptom, while others may have many.

The most noticeable signs of Cushing's Disease include:

* **Urinating frequently and possible urinary incontinence**
* **A pot belly**
* **Drinking excessive amounts of water**
* **A ravenous appetite**
* **Hair loss or recurring skin problems**
* **Thin skin**
* **Muscle wastage**
* **Lack of energy, general lethargy**
* **Panting a lot**

Causes and Outcomes

There are three types of Cushing's Disease, each of which has a different cause. Identifying the cause is important because the various types of the disease are treated differently and each has a different prognosis.

Some 85% to 90% of all cases are caused by a tumour of the pituitary gland located at the base of the brain. Usually benign and often very small, this tumour puts pressure on the pituitary gland, causing an increase in its secretion. This then causes the adrenal gland to release additional cortisol.

Generally if the activity of the adrenal gland can be controlled, many dogs with this form of Cushing's can live normal lives for many years, as long as they take their medication and are closely supervised. However, if the tumour grows it will affect the brain, giving the pet a less favourable prognosis. This happens in around 15% of these cases.

The second type is caused by a benign or malignant tumour of the adrenal gland. If it is benign, it can be removed by surgery. If malignant, surgery may help for some time, but the prognosis is not as good.

In the third type - called iatrogenic Cushing's Disease- the over-use of steroids (artificial hormones), such as Cortisone, Prednisone and others can lead to the disease. Although the steroids were usually given for a legitimate medical reason, they have resulted in an excess and this has a detrimental effect on the dog.

Treatment

A number of tests are necessary to diagnose and confirm Cushing's Disease. The two most common ones are the ACTH stimulation test (see

157

our section on **Addison's Disease**) and the LDDS test. Your vet may also recommend an abdominal ultrasound.

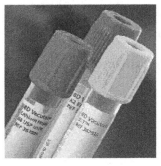

Cushing's Disease cannot be cured, but it can be managed and controlled with medication, usually giving your dog a longer, happier life. Lysodren (Mitotane) is the drug of choice for treating the most common pituitary-dependent Cushing's Disease.

Lisodren is similar to chemotherapy; it can have some serious side effects and must be carefully monitored, especially at the beginning. The medication has to be given for the rest of the dog's life.

If you suspect your Labradoodle does have Cushing's Disease, contact your vet immediately.

Epilepsy

Thanks to www.canineepilepsy.co.uk for assistance with this article. If your Labradoodle has epilepsy, we recommend reading this excellent website to gain a greater understanding of the illness.

If you have witnessed your dog having a seizure (convulsion), you will know how frightening it can be. Seizures are not uncommon in dogs, but many dogs have only a single seizure. If your dog has had more than one seizure it may be that he or she is epileptic. Just as in people, there are medications for dogs to control seizures, allowing your dog to live a more normal life.

'Epilepsy' means repeated seizures due to abnormal activity in the brain and is caused by an abnormality in the brain itself.

If seizures happen because of a problem somewhere else in the body, such as heart disease (which stops oxygen reaching the brain), this is not epilepsy. Your vet may do tests to try to find the reason for the epilepsy but in many cases no cause can be identified. Epilepsy affects around four in every 100 dogs and in some breeds it can be hereditary.

Symptoms
Some dogs seem to know when they are about to have a seizure and may behave in a certain way. You will come to recognise these signs as meaning that a seizure is likely. Often dogs just seek out their owner's

company and come to sit beside them when one is about to start. Once it does, the dog is unconscious - he cannot hear or respond to you. Most dogs become stiff, fall onto their side and make running movements with their legs. Sometimes they will cry out and may lose control of their bowels or bladder.

Most seizures last between one and three minutes - **it is worth making a note of the time the seizure starts and ends** because it often seems that a seizure goes on for a lot longer than it actually does. After a seizure, dogs behave in different ways. Some dogs just get up and carry on with what they were doing, while others appear dazed and confused for up to 24 hours afterwards.

Most commonly, dogs will be disoriented for only 10 to 15 minutes before returning to their old self. They often have a set pattern of behaviour that they follow - for example going for a drink of water or asking to go outside to the toilet. If your dog has had more than one seizure, you may well start to notice a pattern of behaviour which is typically repeated.

Most seizures occur while the dog is relaxed and resting quietly. It is very rare for a seizure to occur while exercising. Often seizures occur in the evening or at night.

In a few dogs, seizures seem to be triggered by particular events or stress. It is common for a pattern to develop and, should you dog suffer from epilepsy, you will gradually recognise this as specific to your dog.

What Should I Do?

The most important thing is to **stay calm**. Remember that your dog is unconscious during the seizure and is not in pain or distressed. It is likely to be more distressing for you than for him

Make sure that he is not in a position to injure himself, for example by falling down the stairs, but otherwise do not try to interfere with him. Never try to put your hand inside his mouth during a seizure or you are very likely to get bitten.

Seizures can cause damage to the brain and if your dog has repeated

occurrences, it is likely that further seizures will occur in the future. The damage caused is cumulative and after a lot of seizures there may be enough brain damage to cause early senility (with loss of learned behaviour and house-training or behavioural changes). It is very rare for dogs to injure themselves during a seizure. Occasionally they may bite their tongue and there may appear to be a lot of blood, but is unlikely to be serious; your dog will not swallow his tongue.

If it goes on for a very long time (more than 10 minutes), the body temperature will rise and this can cause damage to other organs such as the liver and kidneys as well as the brain. In very extreme cases, some dogs may be left in a coma.

When Should I Contact the Vet?

Generally, if your dog has a seizure lasting more than five minutes, or is having more than three a day, you should contact your vet. When your dog starts a seizure, make a note of the time. If he comes out of it within five minutes, then allow him time to recover quietly before contacting your vet. This is far better for your dog than bundling him into the car and carting him off to the vet right away.

However, if your dog does not come out of the seizure within five minutes, or has repeated seizures close together, contact your vet immediately, as he or she will want to see him as soon as possible. If this is his first, your vet may ask you to bring him in for a check and some routine blood tests. Always call your vet's practice before setting off to be sure that there is someone there who can help your dog.

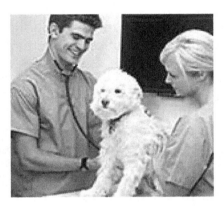

There are many things other than epilepsy which cause seizures in dogs. When your vet first examines your dog, he or she will not know whether your dog has epilepsy or another illness.

It's unlikely that the vet will see your dog during a seizure, so it is vital that you're able to describe in some detail just what happens. You might want to make notes or take a video on your mobile phone. Epilepsy usually starts when the dog is aged between one and five. So if your dog is older or younger, it's more likely he has a different problem.

The vet may need to run a battery of tests to ensure that there is no other cause. These may include blood tests, possibly X-rays and maybe even a scan (MRI) of your dog's brain. If no other cause can be found, then a diagnosis of epilepsy may be made.
If your Labradoodle already has epilepsy, remember these key points:

*Don't change or stop any medication without consulting your vet.
*See your vet at least once a year for follow-up visits.
*Be sceptical of 'magic cure' treatments.

Remember, live *with* epilepsy not *for* epilepsy. With proper medical treatment, most epileptic dogs have far more good days than bad ones. Enjoy all those good days.

Treatment

It is not usually possible to remove the cause of the seizures, so your vet will use medication to control them. This treatment will not cure the disease, but merely manage the signs – even a well-controlled epileptic will have occasional seizures. Sadly, as yet there is no miracle cure for epilepsy, so don't be tempted with 'instant cures' from the internet.

There are many drugs used in the control of epilepsy in people, but very few of these are suitable for long-term use in a dog. Many epileptic dogs require a combination of one or more types of drug to achieve the most effective control of their seizures. Treatment is decided on an individual basis and it may take some time to find the best combination and dose of drugs for your pet. You must have patience when managing an epileptic pet.

It is important that medication is given at the same time each day. Once your dog has been on treatment for a while, he will become dependent on the levels of drug in his blood at all times to control seizures. If you miss a dose of treatment, blood levels can drop and this may be enough to trigger a seizure.

Each epileptic dog is an individual and a treatment plan will be designed specifically for him. It will be based on the severity and frequency of the seizures and how they respond to different medications.

Keep a record of events in your dog's life, note down dates and times of seizures and record when you have given medication. Each time you visit your vet, take this diary along with you so he or she can see how your pet has been since their last check-up. If seizures are becoming more frequent, it may be necessary to change the medication. The success or otherwise of treatment may depend on you keeping a close eye on your dog to see if there are any physical or behavioural changes.

It is rare for epileptic dogs to stop having seizures altogether. However, provided your dog is checked regularly by your vet to make sure that the drugs are not causing any side-effects, there is a good chance that he will live a full and happy life.

Visit **www.canineepilepsy.co.uk** for more information.

Heart Problems

Tricuspid Valve Dysplasia (TVD) is a cardiac defect that affects some Labradors. It is congenital - dogs are born with it - and inherited. Because it is present in some Labradors, it may affect a small percentage of Labradoodles, of whatever cross.

The tricuspid valve is one of four heart valves and if a puppy inherits the TVD gene - or genes this valve will be malformed. It will not form a tight seal, allowing blood to leak and flow back the wrong way. A puppy may be mildly or severely affected, in mild cases, the dog will life a normal life span.

Symptoms
This problem may not be obvious, but some signs to look out for are fluid retention (usually noticed as unexplained weight gain), cool extremities and an intolerance to exercise. Many dogs however, will exhibit no signs until heart failure occurs.

Diagnosis
Any leak from a faulty valve significant enough to cause health problems should be found by a physical exam. Usually a heart murmur will be heard with a stethoscope, although with extremely mild cases, this may not be so.

Occasionally the leak will be so large that it can be felt by hand on the right side of the chest; this is known as a *'thrill'*.

If a heart murmur or thrill is detected in a young dog, your vet will perform chest x-rays and an ultrasound of the heart (echocardiogram) to confirm the diagnosis and extent of the problem. There are other congenital heart problems besides TVD, so a full cardiac examination is important to identify the exact problem.

Treatment
There is currently no cure for TVV, and treatment will depend on how the severity of the condition. Mild cases may require no treatment whatsoever. More severe cases will be treated according to the symptoms. This normally includes the prescription of diuretics, which help remove excess water from the body, and digitalis, which strengthens the heart's contractions. Your vet may also recommend a low salt diet and restrictions on exercise. Following you vet's advice will help your dog to live a healthy life for longer.

Canine Diabetes

This is not an issue which particularly affects Labradoodles any more than any other type of dog, but can affect dogs of all breeds, sizes and both genders.

There are two types: ***diabetes mellitus*** and ***diabetes insipidus***. Diabetes mellitus is the most common form and affects one in 500 dogs. Labradoodles are regarded as having a moderate risk of contracting this. Thanks to modern veterinary medicine, the condition is now treatable and need not shorten your Labradoodle's lifespan or interfere with his quality of life.

Diabetic dogs undergoing treatment now have the same life expectancy as non-diabetic dogs of the same age and gender. However, if left untreated, the disease can lead to cataracts, increasing weakness in the legs (neuropathy), other ailments and even death. In dogs, diabetes is typically seen anywhere between the ages of four to 14, with a peak at seven to nine years. Both males and females can develop it; unspayed females have a slightly higher risk. The typical canine diabetes sufferer is middle-aged, female and overweight, but there are also juvenile cases.

What is Diabetes?

Diabetes insipidus is caused by a lack of vasopressin, a hormone which controls the kidneys' absorption of water.

Diabetes mellitus occurs when the dog's body does not produce enough insulin and cannot successfully process sugars.

Dogs, like us, get their energy by converting the food they eat into sugars, mainly glucose. This glucose travels in the dog's bloodstream and individual cells then remove some of that glucose from the blood to use for energy. The substance that allows the cells to take glucose from the blood is a protein called *insulin*.

Insulin is created by beta cells that are located in the pancreas, which is next to the stomach. Almost all diabetic dogs have Type 1 diabetes: their pancreas does not produce any insulin. Without it, the cells have no way to use the glucose that is in the bloodstream, so the cells 'starve' while the glucose level in the blood rises.

Your vet will use blood samples and urine samples to check glucose concentrations in order to diagnose diabetes. Early treatment helps to prevent further complications developing.

Symptoms

The most common symptoms of diabetes in dogs include:

*Extreme thirst
*Excessive urination
*Weight loss
*Increased appetite
*Coat in poor condition
*Lethargy
*Vision problems due to cataracts

Cataracts and Diabetes

Some diabetic dogs do go blind. Cataracts may develop due to high blood glucose levels causing water to build up in the eyes' lenses. This leads to swelling, rupture of the lens fibres and the development of cataracts. In many cases, the cataracts can be surgically removed to bring sight back to the dog. Vision is restored in 75% to 80% of diabetic dogs that undergo cataract removal.

However, some dogs may stay blind even after the cataracts are gone, and some cataracts simply cannot be removed. Blind dogs are often able to get around surprisingly well, particularly in a familiar home.

Treatment

Treatment starts with the right diet. Your vet will prescribe meals low in fat and sugars. He will also recommend medication. Many cases of canine diabetes can be successfully treated with diet and medication. More severe cases may require insulin injections. In the newly-diagnosed dog, insulin therapy begins at home.

Normally, after a week of treatment, you return to the vet who will do a series of blood sugar tests over a 12-14 hour period to see when the blood glucose peaks and when it hits its lows. Adjustments are then made to the dosage and timing of the injections. Your vet will explain how to prepare and inject the insulin. You may be asked to collect urine samples using a test strip (a small piece of paper that indicates the glucose levels in urine).

If your dog is already having insulin injections, beware of a 'miracle cure' offered on some internet sites. It does not exist. There is no diet or vitamin supplement which can reduce your dog's dependence on insulin injections because vitamins and minerals cannot do what insulin does in the dog's body. If you think that your dog needs a supplement, discuss it with your vet first to make sure that it does not interfere with any other medication.

Exercise

Managing your dog's diabetes also means managing his activity level. Exercise burns up blood glucose the same way that insulin does. If your dog is on insulin, any active exercise on top of the insulin might cause him to have a severe low blood glucose episode, called 'hypoglycaemia'.

Keep your dog on a reasonably consistent exercise routine. Your usual insulin dose will take that amount of exercise into account.

If you plan to take your dog out for some extra demanding exercise, such as swimming or playing in the snow, give him only half of his usual insulin dose.

Tips

- You can usually buy specially formulated diabetes dog food from your veterinarian

- You should feed the same type and amount of food at the same time every day

- Most veterinarians recommend twice a day feeding for diabetic pets. It is OK if your dog prefers to eat more often

"I DON'T SEE TABLE SCRAPS."

- If you have other pets in the home, they should also be placed on a twice-a-day feeding schedule, so that the diabetic dog cannot eat from their bowls. Help your dog to achieve the best possible blood glucose control by not feeding him table scraps or treats between meals

Watch for signs that your dog is starting to drink more water than usual. Call the vet if you see this happening, as it may mean that the insulin dose needs adjusting.

Remember these simple points:

Food raises blood glucose
Insulin and exercise lower blood glucose
Keep them in balance

A website with more information on canine diabetes can be found at **www.caninediabetes.org**

_____

Canine Cancer

This is the biggest single killer of dogs of whatever breed and will claim the lives of one in four dogs. It is the cause of nearly half the deaths of all dogs aged 10 years and older, according to the American Veterinary Medical Association.

Symptoms

Early detection is critical. Some things to look out for are:

*Swellings anywhere on the body
*Lumps in a dog's armpit or under his jaw
*Sores that don't heal
*Bad breath
*Weight loss
*Poor appetite, difficulty swallowing or excessive drooling
*Changes in exercise or stamina level
*Laboured breathing
*Change in bowel or bladder habits

If your dog has been spayed or neutered, the risk of certain cancers decreases. These cancers include uterine and breast/mammary cancer in females, and testicular cancer in males (if the dog was neutered before he was six months old).

Along with controlling the pet population, spaying is especially important because mammary cancer in female dogs is fatal in about 50% of all cases.

Diagnosis

Just because your dog has a skin growth doesn't mean that it's cancerous. As with humans, tumours may be benign (harmless) or malignant (harmful).

Your vet will probably confirm the tumour using X-rays, blood tests and possibly ultrasounds. He or she will then decide whether it is benign or malignant via a biopsy in which a tissue sample is taken from your dog and examined under a microscope.

If your dog is diagnosed with cancer, there is hope. Advances in veterinary medicine and technology offer various treatment options, including chemotherapy, radiation and surgery. Unlike with humans, a dog's hair will not fall out with chemotherapy.

Treatment

Canine cancer is growing at an ever-increasing rate. One of the difficulties is that your pet cannot tell you when a cancer is developing, but if cancers can be detected early enough through a physical or behavioural change, they often respond well to treatment.

Over recent years, we have all become more aware of the risk factors for human cancer. Responding to these by changing our habits is having a significant impact on human health. For example, stopping smoking, protecting ourselves from over-exposure to strong sunlight and eating a healthy, balanced diet all help to reduce cancer rates. We know to keep a close eye on ourselves, go for regular health checks and report any lumps and bumps to our doctors as soon as they appear. Increased cancer awareness is definitely improving human health.

The same is true with your dog. While it is impossible to completely prevent cancer from occurring, a healthy lifestyle with a balanced diet and plenty of exercise can help to reduce the risk. Also, be aware of any new lumps and bumps on your dog's body and any changes in his behaviour.

The success of treatment will depend on the type of cancer, the treatment used and on how early the tumour is found. The sooner treatment begins, the greater the chances of success. One of the best things you can do for your dog is to keep a close eye on him for any tell-tale signs.

This shouldn't be too difficult and can be done as part of your regular handling and grooming. If you notice any new bumps, for example, monitor them over a period of days to see if there is a change in their appearance or size. If there is, then make an appointment to see your vet as soon as possible. It might only be a cyst, but better to be safe than sorry.

The Future

Research into earlier diagnosis and improved treatments is being conducted at veterinary schools and companies all over the world. Advances in biology are producing a steady flow of new tests and treatments which are now becoming available to improve survival rates and canine cancer care.

If your dog is diagnosed with cancer. Do not despair, there are many options and new, improved treatments are constantly being introduced.

Our Happy Ending

We know from personal experience that canine cancer can be successfully treated if it is diagnosed early enough. Our dog Max was diagnosed with T-cell lymphoma when he was four years old. We had noticed a black lump on his anus which grew to the size of a small grape.

We took him to the vet within the first few days of seeing the lump and, after a test, he was diagnosed with the dreaded T-cell lymphoma. This is a particularly nasty and aggressive form of cancer which can spread to the lymph system and is often fatal for dogs.

As soon as the diagnosis was confirmed our vet Graham operated on Max and removed the lump. He also had to remove one of his anal glands, but as dogs have two, this was not a serious worry. Afterwards, we were on tenterhooks, not knowing if another lump would grow or if the cancer had already spread to his lymph system.

After a few months, Max had another blood test and was finally given the all-clear. Max is now happy, healthy and nine years old. We were very lucky. I would strongly advise anyone who suspects that their dog has cancer to get him or her to your local vet as soon as possible.

10. Labradoodle Skin

A whole book could be written on this subject alone. As with the human population, skin conditions, allergies and intolerances appear to be on the increase in the canine world.

While many Labradoodles have no problems at all, some suffer from sensitive skin, allergies or skin disorders, causing them to scratch, bite or lick themselves excessively on the feet and/or other areas. Symptoms may vary from mild itchiness to a chronic reaction.

Canine skin disorders are a complex topic. Some dogs can spend hours running through fields, digging holes and rolling around in the grass with no after-effects at all. Others may spend most of their time indoors and have an excellent diet, but still experience severe itching.

Skin conditions may be the result of one or more of a wide range of causes - and the list of potential remedies and treatments is even longer. It's by no means possible to cover all of them in this chapter. Our aim is to give a broad outline of some of the ailments most likely to affect Labradoodles We have also included remedies tried with some success by ourselves (our dog has skin issues) and other owners of dogs with skin problems.

This information is not intended to take the place of professional help. We are not animal health experts and you should always contact your veterinarian when your dog appears physically unwell or uncomfortable. This is particularly true with skin conditions. A vet may be able to find the source of the problem early on and treat it successfully before it develops into anything more serious for your Labradoodle.

One of the difficulties with this type of ailment is that the exact cause is often difficult to diagnose, as the symptoms may be common to other ailments as well. If allergies are involved, some specific tests are available costing hundreds of pounds or dollars. You will have to take your vet's advice on this, as the tests are not always conclusive and if the answer is grass or dust, it's impossible to keep your dog away from the triggers while still having a normal life.

It is often a question of managing the problem, rather than curing it.

Skin issues and allergies often develop in adolescence or early adulthood. Our dog Max was perfectly normal until he reached two years old when he began scratching, caused by environmental allergies, most likely pollen. He's now nine and over the years he's been on various different remedies which have all worked for a time.

As his allergies are seasonal, he normally does not have any medication between October and March. But come spring and as sure as daffodils are daffodils, he starts scratching again. Luckily, they are manageable and Max lives a happy, normal life.

Another issue reported by some Labradoodle owners is food allergy or intolerance (there is a difference). Whatever the cause, before a vet can diagnose the problem, you have to be prepared to tell him or her all about your dog's diet, exercise regime, habits, medical history and local environment. The vet will then carry out a thorough physical examination, possibly followed by further tests, before a course of treatment can be prescribed.

We'll start with one of the rarest skin problems, but one which can be inherited by Labradoodles, and that is Sebaceous Adenitis, or SA.

Sebaceous Adenitis

This is a rare inflammatory skin disease that affects the skin glands of young and middle age dogs. It most commonly affects Poodles, Akitas

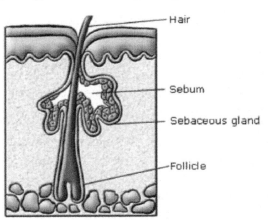

and Samoyeds, although other breeds (and some cats and horses) can also be infected. Sebaceous glands are microscopic glands found below the skin which secrete an oily substance (sebum) to lubricate the dog's skin and hair.

SA is a type of autoimmune disease where the dog's sebaceous glands become inflamed and are eventually destroyed. The exact cause is as yet unknown and is the subject of current research. The diagram shows a normal sebaceous gland.

There are two types of the condition - one for long or double coated breeds, such as the Poodle, and one for short coated breeds - each has different symptoms.

170

Symptoms

For Poodles and Labradoodles, these are:

- Alopecia (hair loss), often in a circular pattern
- Silvery scales or dandruff which sticks to the fur
- A rancid or musty odour
- Matted hair
- Dull, brittle or coarse hair
- Intense itching and scratching
- Bacterial infections along the hair follicle
- Skin lesions on the head or back

There is a bi-annual test for sebaceous adenitis, which is recommended for Labradoodles of F2 generation and higher and backcrosses (Bs).

Diagnosis

One of the problems with diagnosis is that there are a number of other conditions with similar symptoms. These include **Seborrhoea**, where the dog's body produces keratin, which results in flaking and itching of the skin; **Demodicosis,** an overgrowth of skin mites that can cause itching, hair loss and swelling; **Dermatophytosis**, a fungal infection which also causes itching and flaking, and **Endocrine Skin Disease.** To test for SA, a vet may take skin scrapings and endocrine function tests and usually a skin biopsy.

Treatment

There is no cure and treatment is generally lifelong. It usually involves regular bathing with antiseborrheic shampoos (such as Malaseb), soaking in mineral oils, giving fatty acid supplements and, in more in more severe cases, the prescription of steroids.

Types of Allergies

'Canine dermatitis' means inflammation of a dog's skin and it can be triggered by numerous things, but the most common by far is allergies.

Symptoms

- Chewing on feet
- Rubbing the face on the carpet
- Scratching the body
- Recurrent ear infections
- Hair loss
- Mutilated skin

A dog who is allergic to something will show it through skin problems and itching, your vet may call this *'pruritus'*. It may seem logical that if a dog is allergic to something he inhales, like certain pollen grains, his nose will run, if he's allergic to something he eats, he may vomit, or if allergic to an insect bite, he may develop a swelling. But in practice this is seldom the case. Instead, he will have a mild to severe itching sensation over his body and maybe a chronic ear infection.

Dogs with allergies often chew their feet until they are sore and red. They may rub their faces on the carpet or couch or scratch their belly and sides. Because the ear glands produce too much wax in response to the allergy, ear infections can occur, and bacteria and yeast often thrive in the excessive wax and debris.

An allergic dog may cause skin lesions by constant chewing and scratching. Sometimes he will lose hair, which can be patchy or inconsistent over the body leaving a mottled appearance. The skin itself may be dry and crusty, reddened or oily, depending on the dog. It is very common to get secondary bacterial skin infections due to these self-inflicted wounds. An allergic dog's body is reacting to certain molecules called 'allergens.' These may come from:

- Trees
- Grass
- Pollens
- Fabrics such as wool or nylon
- Rubber and plastics
- Foods and food additives, such as individual meats, grains or colourings
- Milk products
- House dust and dust mites
- Flea bites

These allergens may be **inhaled** as the dog breathes, **ingested** as the dog eats or caused by **contact** with the dog's body when he walks or

rolls. However they arrive, they all cause the immune system to produce a protein (IgE), which causes various irritating chemicals, such as histamine, to be released. In dogs these chemical reactions and cell types occur in sizeable amounts only within the skin.

A tendency to have allergies can be passed from generation to generation within breeds. Examples are terriers such as the Scottish, West Highland

White, Cairn and Wire-Haired Fox, as well as Lhasa Apso, Pug, Miniature Schnauzer and English Bulldog.

Among the larger breeds, English and Irish Setters, Retrievers and Dalmatians can be affected.

Inhalant Allergies (Atopy)

The most common allergies are inhalant and seasonal (at least at first, some allergies may develop and worsen). Substances which can cause an allergic reaction in dogs are similar to those causing problems for some humans and include pollens, trees, other animals, dust mites and mould.

A clue to diagnosing these allergies is to look at the timing of the reaction. Does it happen all year round? If so, this may be mould or dust. If the reaction is seasonal, then pollens may well be the culprit.

A diagnosis can be made by allergy testing - either a blood or intradermal skin test where a small amount of antigen is injected into the dog's skin to test for a reaction. The blood test can give false positives, so the skin test is many veterinarians' preferred method.

Whether or not you take this route will be your decision; allergy testing is not cheap, it takes time and may require your dog to be sedated. There's also no point doing it if you are not going to go along with the recommended method of treatment, which is immunotherapy, or 'hyposensitisation', and this can also be an expensive process.

It consists of a series of injections made specifically for your dog and administered over weeks or months to make him more tolerant of allergens. It may have to be done by a veterinary dermatologist if your vet is not familiar with the treatment.

Veterinarians in the USA claim that success rates can be as high as 75% of cases. Both these tests work best when carried out during the season when the allergies are at their worst.

But before you get to this stage, your vet will have had to rule out other potential causes, such as fleas or mites, fungal, yeast or bacterial infections and hypothyroidism. Due to the time and cost involved in skin testing, most mild cases of allergies are treated with a combination of avoidance, fatty acids and antihistamines.

Environmental or Contact Irritations

These are a direct reaction to something the dog physically comes into contact with. It could be as simple as grass, specific plants, dust or other animals.

If the trigger is grass or other outdoor materials, the allergies are often seasonal. The dog may require treatment (often tablets, shampoo or localised cortisone spray) for spring and summer, but be perfectly fine with no medication for the other half of the year. This is the case with our dog.

Other possible triggers include dry carpet shampoos, caustic irritants, new carpets, cement dust, washing powders or fabric conditioners. If you wash your dog's bedding or if he sleeps on your bed, use a fragrance-free laundry detergent and fabric conditioner.

The irritation may be restricted to the part of the dog - such as the underneath of the paws or belly - which has touched the offending object. Symptoms are skin irritation - either a general problem or specific hotspots - itching (your vet may call this "pruritis") and sometimes hair loss. Readers sometimes report to us that their dog will incessantly lick one part of the body, often the paws, bottom, belly or back.

Diet and Food Allergies

Food is the third most common cause of allergies in dogs, after flea bites and inhalant allergies. There is some anecdotal evidence that food allergies are on the increase within the Labradoodle population.

Cheap dog foods bulked up with grains and other ingredients can cause problems. Some Labradoodle owners have reported their dogs having problems with wheat and other grains. If you feed your dog a dry commercial dog food, make sure that it's a high quality, preferably hypoallergenic, one and that the first ingredient listed on the sack is meat or poultry and not grain.

174

There is also evidence from owners that dogs with nutritional skin problems can do well on a purely vegetarian diet. Another option is to consider putting your Labradoodle on a high protein pure meat diet. Both of these options are expensive and time-consuming for the owner, but can have impressive results in some cases.

Without the correct food a dog's whole body - not just his skin and coat - will continuously be under stress and this manifests itself in a number of ways. The symptoms of food allergies are similar to those of most allergies:

- itchy skin affecting primarily the face, feet, ears, forelegs, armpits and anus
- excessive scratching
- chronic or recurring ear infections
- hair loss
- hot spots
- skin infections that clear up with antibiotics but return after the antibiotics have finished
- possible increased bowel movements, maybe twice as many as normal

The bodily process which occurs when an animal has a reaction to a particular food agent is not very well understood, but the veterinary profession does know how to diagnose and treat food allergies. As many other problems can cause similar symptoms to food allergies (and also the fact that many sufferers also have other allergies), it is important that any other problems are identified and treated before food allergies are diagnosed.

Atopy, flea bite allergies, intestinal parasite hypersensitivities, sarcoptic mange and yeast or bacterial infections can all cause similar symptoms. This can be an anxious time for owners as vets try one thing after another to get to the bottom of the allergy.

The normal method for diagnosing a food allergy is elimination. Once all other causes have been ruled out or treated, then a food trial is the next step – and that's no picnic for owners either. See our **Chapter 5. Feeding** for more information on canine food allergies and what to feed your dog. The treatment for food allergies is to avoid feeding the ingredients which trigger the reaction. Once these have been identified, perhaps through a food trial (which is often easier said than done), they can be eliminated from the diet.

As with other allergies, dogs may have short-term relief by taking fatty acids, antihistamines, and steroids, but removing the offending items from the diet is the only permanent solution.

Flea Bite Allergies
These are the most common canine allergy and affect dogs of all breeds. To compound the problem, many dogs with flea allergies also have inhalant allergies. Flea bite allergy is typically seasonal, worse during summer and autumn – peak time for fleas - and is worse in climates where fleas are prevalent.

This type of allergy is not to the flea itself, but to proteins in flea saliva, which are deposited under the dog's skin when the insect feeds. Just one bite in an allergic Labradoodle will cause intense and long-lasting itching. If affected, a dog will bite at the base of his tail and scratch a lot. Most of the damage is done by the dog scratching, rather than the flea bite, and can result in the dog's hair dropping out or skin abrasions.

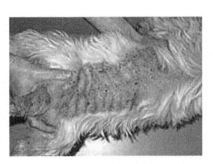

Some dogs will develop round, red, painful sores called hot spots. These can occur anywhere, but are often along the back and base of the tail. Flea bite allergies can only be totally prevented by keeping all fleas away from the dog. Various flea prevention treatments are available – see our next section on Parasites. If you suspect your dog may be allergic to fleas, consult your veterinarian for the proper diagnosis and medication.

Other Skin Problems

Parasites
Fleas - When you see your dog scratching and biting, your first thought is probably: "He's got fleas!" and you may well be right. Fleas don't fly, but they do have very strong back legs and they will take any opportunity to jump from the ground or another animal into your Labradoodle's lovely warm coat. You can sometimes see the fleas if you part your dog's fur.

And for every flea that you see on your pet, there is the awful prospect of hundreds of eggs and larvae in your house and garden. So if your Labradoodle is unlucky enough to catch fleas, you'll have to treat your environment as well as your dog order to completely get rid of them.

The best form of cure is prevention. Vets recommend giving dogs a preventative flea treatment every four to eight weeks. This may vary depending on your climate, the season (fleas do not breed as quickly in the cold) and how much time your dog spends outdoors.

Once-a-month topical (applied to the skin) insecticides - like Frontline and Advantix - are the most commonly used flea prevention products on the market. You part the skin and apply drops of the liquid on to a small area on your pet's back, usually near the neck. Some kill fleas and ticks, and others just kill fleas, check the details.

It is worth spending the money on a quality treatment, as cheaper brands may not rid your Labradoodle completely of fleas, ticks and other parasites. Sprays, dips, shampoos and collars are other options, as are tablets and injections in certain cases, such as before your dog goes into boarding kennels or has surgery. Incidentally, a flea bite is different from a flea bite allergy.

NOTE: There is considerable anecdotal evidence from dog owners of various breeds that the flea and worm tablet **Trifexis,** available in the USA, may cause severe side effects in some dogs. You may wish to read some owners' experiences at: www.max-the-schnauzer.com/trifexis-side-effects-in-schnauzers.html

Ticks – A tick (left) is not an insect, but a member of the arachnid family, like the spider. There are over 850 types of them, divided into two types: hard shelled and soft shelled.

Ticks don't have wings - they can't fly, they crawl. They have a sensor called 'Haller's organ' which detects smell, heat and humidity to help them locate food, which in some cases is a Labradoodle. A tick's diet consists of one thing and one thing only – blood! They climb up onto tall grass and when they sense an animal is close, crawl on him.

Ticks can pass on a number of diseases to animals and humans, the most well-known of which is Lyme Disease, a serious condition which causes lameness and other problems. Dogs which spend a lot of time outdoors in woods regarded as high risk areas can have a vaccination against Lime Disease. If you do find a tick on your Labradoodle's coat it is recommended that you have it removed by a vet. Pulling it

out yourself and leaving a bit of the tick behind can be detrimental to your dog's health.

Prevention treatment is similar to that for fleas. If your Labradoodle has particularly sensitive skin, he might do better with a natural flea or tick remedy.

Ringworm -This is not actually a worm, but a fungus and is most commonly seen in puppies and young dogs. It is highly infectious and often found on the face, ears, paws or tail. The ringworm fungus is most prevalent in hot, humid climates, but surprisingly, most cases occur in the autumn and winter. Ringworm infections in dogs are not that common, in one study of dogs with active skin problems, less than 3% had ringworm.

Ringworm is transmitted by spores in the soil and by contact with the infected hair of dogs and cats, which can be typically found on carpets, brushes, combs, toys and furniture. Spores from infected animals can be shed into the environment and live for over 18 months, but fortunately most healthy adult dogs have some resistance and never develop symptoms.

The fungi live in dead skin, hairs and nails and the head and legs are the most common areas affected. Tell-tale signs are bald patches with a roughly circular shape (see photo) Ringworm is usually treated with fungicidal shampoos or antibiotics from a vet.

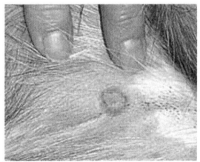 Humans can catch ringworm from pets, and vice versa. Children are especially susceptible, as are adults with suppressed immune systems and those undergoing chemotherapy. Hygiene is extremely important, if you have a dog with ringworm, wear gloves when handling him and wash your hands well afterwards. And if a member of your family catches ringworm, make sure they use separate towels from everyone else or the fungus may spread.

Sarcoptic Mange
Also known as canine scabies, this is caused by the parasite *Sarcoptes scabiei*. This microscopic mite can cause a range of skin problems, the most common of which is hair loss and severe itching. The mites can infect other animals such as foxes, cats and even humans, but prefer to live their short lives on dogs. Fortunately, there are several good treatments for this mange and the disease can be easily controlled.

In cool, moist environments, they live for up to 22 days. At normal room temperature they live from two to six days, preferring to live on parts of the dog with less hair. These are the areas you may see him scratching, although it can spread throughout the body in severe cases.

Diagnosing canine scabies can be somewhat difficult, and it is often mistaken for inhalant allergies. Once diagnosed, there are a number of effective treatments, including selamectin (Revolution), a topical solution applied once a month which also provides heartworm prevention, flea control, some tick protection and protection against Sarcoptic mange. Various Frontline Frontline products are also effective – check with your vet for the correct ones.

Because your dog does not have to come into direct contact with an infected dog to catch scabies, it is difficult to completely protect him. Foxes and their environment can also transmit the mite, so keep your dog away from areas where you know foxes are present.

Bacterial infection (Pyoderma)

Pyoderma literally means 'pus in the skin' (yuk!) and fortunately this condition is not contagious. Early signs of this bacterial infection are itchy red spots filled with yellow pus, similar to pimples or spots in humans. They can sometimes develop into red, ulcerated skin with dry and crusty patches.

Pyoderma is caused by several things: a broken skin surface, a skin wound due to chronic exposure to moisture, altered skin bacteria, or impaired blood flow to the skin. Dogs have a higher risk of developing an infection when they have a fungal infection or an endocrine (hormone gland) disease such as hyperthyroidism, or have allergies to fleas, food ingredients or parasites.

Pyoderma is often secondary to allergic dermatitis and develops in the lesions on the skin which happen as a result of scratching. Puppies often develop 'puppy pyoderma' in thinly-haired areas such as the groin and underarms. Fleas, ticks, yeast or fungal skin infections, thyroid disease, hormonal imbalances, heredity and some medications can increase the risk.

If you notice symptoms, get your dog to the vet quickly before the condition develops from superficial pyoderma into severe pyoderma, which is much more unpleasant and takes a lot longer to treat.

Bacterial infection, no matter how bad it may look, usually responds well to medical treatment, which is generally done on an outpatient basis. Superficial pyoderma will usually be treated with a two to six-week course of antibiotic tablets or ointment. Severe or recurring pyoderma looks awful, causes your dog some distress and can take two or three months' of treatment to completely cure. Medicated shampoos and regular bathing, as instructed by your vet, are also part of the treatment. It's important to ensure your dog has clean, dry, padded bedding.

Ear Infections

Infection of the external ear canal (outer ear infection) is called otitis externa and is one of the most common types of infections seen in dogs. Some breeds, particularly those with large, floppy or hairy ears like Cocker Spaniels, Miniature Poodles or Old English Sheepdogs, appear to be more prone to this painful condition, as are certain Labradoodles.

Many dogs with chronic or recurring ear infections have inhalant or food allergies or low thyroid function (hypothyroidism). Sometimes the ears are the first sign of allergy. The underlying problem must be treated or the dog will continue to have chronic ear problems. Tell-tale signs include your dog shaking his head, scratching his ears a lot, or an unpleasant odour coming from the ears.

If you look under his ear flap, you may notice it is red and inflamed with a lot of wax or discharge. He may also appear depressed or irritable; this is because ear infections are painful. In chronic cases, the inside of his ears may become crusty or thickened.

Dogs can have ear problems for many different reasons, including:

- Allergies such as atopy or food allergies
- Ear mites or other parasites
- Bacteria or yeast infections
- Injury, often due to excessive scratching
- Hormonal abnormalities, e.g. hypothyroidism
- The ear anatomy and environment, e.g. excess moisture
- Hereditary or immune conditions and tumours

Treatment depends on the cause of the ear problem and what other conditions your dog may have. Antibiotics are used for bacterial infections and antifungals for yeast infections. Glucocorticoids, such as dexamethasone, are often included in these medications to reduce the inflammation in the ear.

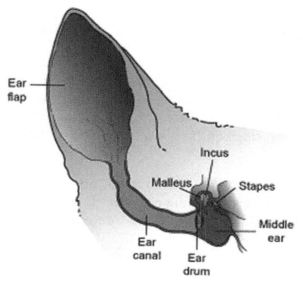

A dog's ear canal is L-shaped, which means it can be difficult to get medication into the lower (horizontal) part of the ear. The best method is to hold the dog's ear flap with one hand and put the ointment or drops in with the other, if possible tilting the dog's head away from you so the liquid flows downwards.

Make sure you then hold the ear flap down and massage the medication into the horizontal canal before letting go of your dog, as the first thing he will do is shake his head.

Nearly all ear infections can be successfully managed if properly diagnosed and treated. But if an underlying problem remains undiscovered, the outcome will be less favourable. Deep ear infections can damage or rupture the eardrum, causing an internal ear infection and even permanent hearing loss.

Closing of the ear canal (*hyperplasia* or *stenosis*) is another sign of severe infection. Most extreme cases of hyperplasia will eventually require surgery as a last resort; the most common procedure is called a *lateral ear resection*.

Following numerous ear infections - and despite regularly cleaning his ears and having them plucked at the groomer's – our Max had this operation. It really was the last-resort option as it is extremely painful for the dog, but it was that or risk him going deaf, according to the vet.

Max had the operation 10 months ago and so far (touch wood) it has worked and he has been ear infection-free. However, I would not advise the operation unless your vet strongly recommends it.

The key to healthy ears is to keep them clean. Check your dog's ears and clean them once to three times weekly, especially if your Labradoodle loves swimming, as many do. One of the problems with particularly furry ears is that the air cannot circulate, so if you know your dog is prone to ear infections, it is good practice to regularly pluck or clip excess hair to allow air to flow more freely.

If your dog appears to be in pain, has smelly ears or if his ear canals look inflamed, contact your vet straight away. If he has a ruptured or weakened eardrum, ear cleansers and medications could do more harm than good.

Hormonal Imbalances

These are often difficult to diagnose and occur when the dog is producing either too much (hyper) or too little (hypo) of a particular hormone. One visual sign is often hair loss on both sides of the dog's body. The condition is not usually itchy.

Hormone imbalances can be serious as they are often indicators that glands which affect the dog internally are not working properly. However, some types can be diagnosed by special blood tests and treated effectively.

Some Allergy Treatments

Treatments and success rates vary tremendously from dog to dog and from one allergy to another, which is why it is so important to consult a vet at the outset. Earlier diagnosis is more likely to lead to a successful treatment.

Some owners whose Labradoodles have recurring skin issues find that a course of antibiotics or steroids works wonders for their dog's sore skin and itching. However, the scratching starts all over again when the treatment stops.

While blood and skin tests are available, followed by hypersensitisation treatment, the specific trigger for many dogs with inhalant or contact allergies remains unknown. So the reality for many owners of Labradoodles with allergies is that they manage the ailment with various medications and practices, rather than curing it completely.

Our Personal Experience

After speaking to our vet and corresponding with numerous other dog owners, it seems that our experiences with allergies were not uncommon. Our dog, Max, was perfectly fine until he was about two years old when he began to scratch a lot (he's nine now). He seemed to scratch more in spring and summer, which meant that his allergies were almost certainly inhalant or contact-based and related to pollens, grasses or other outdoor triggers.

One option is to have a barrage of tests on the dog to discover exactly what he is allergic to. We decided not to do this, not because of the cost, but because our vet said it was highly likely that Max is allergic to pollens, and he is an active dog getting three walks a day, mostly in the countryside where we live.

If we had confirmed an allergy to pollens, we were not going to stop taking him outside for walks, so the vet treated him on the basis of seasonal inhalant or contact allergies, probably related to pollen.

One recommendation he makes to reduce the itching is to rinse the dog's paws and underneath his belly after a walk in the countryside. This is something Graham does with his own dogs and has found that the scratching reduces as a result.

Regarding medications, Max was at first put on to a tiny dose of Piriton, an antihistamine for hay fever sufferers (human and canine) and for the first spring and summer, this worked well.

One of the problems with allergies is that they can change and the dog can also build up a tolerance to a treatment – this has been the case over the years with Max. The symptoms change from season to season, although the main symptoms remain and they are general scratching, paw biting and ear infections.

One year he bit the skin under his tail a lot and this was treated fairly effectively with a cortisone spray. This type of spray is useful if the area of itching is localised, but no good for spraying all over a dog's body.

A couple of years ago he started biting his paws for the first time - a habit he persists with - although not to the extent that they become red and raw. Over the years we have tried a number of treatments, all of which have worked for a while, before he comes off the medication in autumn for five or six months when plants and grasses stop growing outdoors. He manages perfectly fine the rest of the year without any medication.

According to our vet, every spring there are more and more dogs appearing in his waiting room with various types of allergies. Whether this is connected to how we breed our dogs remains to be seen. One season he put Max on a short course of steroids. These worked very well for five months, but steroids are not a long-term solution, as prolonged use can cause organ damage.

 Another spring Max was prescribed a non-steroid daily tablet called Atopica, sold in the UK only through vets. This was expensive, but initially extremely effective – so much so that we thought we had cured the problem completely. However, after a couple of seasons on Atopica he developed a tolerance and started scratching again.

Last year went back on the Piriton, a higher dose than when he was two years old, and this worked very well again. One advantage of this drug is that is it manufactured by the million for dogs and is therefore very inexpensive. We also feed him a high quality hypoallergenic dry food. Next spring when Max starts scratching again, we will visit the vet and discuss what treatment will be best. (We'll try and combine it with his annual vaccinations to keep the cost down!)

Many vets recommend adding fish oils (which contain Omega 3 fatty  acids) to a daily feed to keep your dog's skin and coat healthy all year round – whether or not he has problems. We also add a liquid supplement called Yumega Plus, which contains Omega 3 and 6, to one of his two daily feeds all year round and this definitely seems to help his skin.

It also helped his skin to recover after we had to go down the route of a lateral ear resection. When the scratching gets particularly bad, we bathe Max in an antiseborrheic shampoo called Malaseb twice a week, which also seems to help. The only problem with this type of shampoo is that you have to leave it on for 10 minutes before rinsing, not easy with a lively dog.

The main point is that Max's condition is manageable. He still scratches, but not as much as when he was younger. He may have allergies, but he wouldn't miss his walks for anything and all in all, he is one contented canine.

We've compiled some anecdotal evidence from owners of dogs with various allergies, here are some of their suggestions for alleviating the problems:

Bathing - Regularly bathing your dog – anything from twice a week to once every two weeks - using shampoos that break down the oils which plug the hair follicles. These shampoos contain antiseborrheic ingredients such as benzoyl peroxide, salicylic acid, sulfur or tar. One example is

Sulfoxydex shampoo, which can be followed by a cream rinse such as Episoothe Rinse afterwards to prevent the skin from drying out.

Dabbing – Using an astringent such as witch hazel or alcohop on affected areas. We have heard of zinc oxide cream being used to some effect with Labradoodles. In the human world, this is rubbed on to mild skin abrasions and acts as a protective coating. It can help the healing of chapped skin and nappy rash in babies. Zinc oxide works as a mild astringent and has some antiseptic properties and is safe to use on dogs, *as long as you do not allow the dog to lick it off*.

Grooming – Keeping your Labradoodle's coat short. If your dog has particularly hairy ears, (especially smaller minimal-shedding Labradoodles with narrow ear canals) ask the groomer to hand pluck the inside of his ears as part of normal grooming.

Daily supplements - Vitamin E, vitamin A, zinc and omega oils all help to make a dog's skin healthy. Feed a daily supplement which contains some of these, such as fish oil, which provides omega.

 There follows some specific remedies from owners. We are not endorsing them, we're just passing on the information. *Check with your vet before trying any new remedies:*

A medicated shampoo with natural tea tree oil has been suggested by one owner. Some have reported that switching to a fish-based diet has helped lessen scratching. Ann G. said: *"Try Natural Balance Sweet Potato and Fish formula. My dog Charlie has skin issues and this food has helped him tremendously! Plus he LOVES it!"* Others have suggested home-cooked food is best, if you have the time to prepare the food.

This is what another reader had to say: *"My 8-month-old dog also had a contact dermatitis around his neck and chest. I was surprised how extensive it was when I clipped his hair. The vet recommended twice-a-week baths with an oatmeal shampoo. I also applied organic coconut oil daily for a few weeks. This completely cured the dermatitis. I also put a capsule of fish oil with his food once a day and continue to give him twice-weekly baths. His skin is great now."*

Several Labradoodle owners have tried coconut oil with some success. Follow this link for an article on the benefits of coconut oils and fish oils, and why it might be worth considering alternating them. Check with your vet first: www.cocotherapy.com/fishoilsvsvirginoil_coconutoil.htm

And from another reader: *"I have been putting a teaspoon of Canola Oil in my dog's food every other day and it has helped with the itching."* *"I have shampooed the "new" carpet in hopes of removing any of the chemicals that could be irritating her.*
"And I have changed laundry detergent. After several loads of laundry everything has been washed."

Another reader wrote that her dog is being treated for seasonal allergies with half a pill of Claritin a day. Reader Cindi says that local health food stores may be able to offer advice on suitable ingredients for a diet - for dogs as well as humans.

This chapter has only just touched on the complex subject of skin disorders. As you can see, the causes and treatments are many and varied. One thing is true, whatever the condition:

Good quality diet and attention to cleanliness and grooming go a long way in preventing and managing canine skin problems.

If your Labradoodle has a skin issue, seek a professional diagnosis from a veterinarian before attempting to treat the condition.

Early diagnosis and treatment can sometimes alleviate the problem before it develops into anything more serious. Some skin conditions cannot be cured, but they can be successfully managed, allowing your Labradoodle to live a happy, pain-free life.

---

11. Grooming a Labradoodle

Good grooming helps your Doodle look and feel his best. Routine grooming sessions also allow you to examine his coat, teeth, eyes, ears and nails for signs of problems. How much grooming your dog needs depends largely on one factor – what coat he has. There are three different types of coats and then variations within these three.

If your dog has a **hair** coat, it may be straight or wavy and he will most likely shed, but this is the easiest coat of all to care for as your dog will naturally moult. You are more likely to get this type of coat from F1 Labradoodles, especially those puppies which take after the Labrador parent.

The other two types are **wool** and **fleece** and both of these types are regarded as low or minimal shedding – although the degree will vary from one Doodle to another. Australian Labradoodles have one of these types of coat, as well as most other multigeneration Doodles. However, although these dogs are likely to be low or minimal shedding, there is no 100% guarantee that the dog will not shed as this varies from one dog another, even within litters. It may even be that your puppy sheds and the adult dog will not shed so much - or vice versa.

Wool and fleece coats are high maintenance as far as grooming is concerned. You cannot simply leave them unkempt and will have to decide how short to keep your Doodle's coat. If you are experienced you can clipper or hand strip the dog yourself, otherwise it's regular trips to a professional groomer and an additional expense you need to factor in. But whichever way you look at it, a well-groomed Doodle is a joy to behold. Here are some general tips for keeping all Doodles in tip top condition.

Ear cleaning

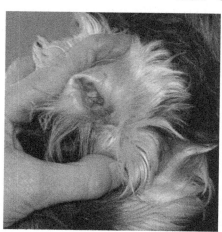

This should be part of your normal at-home grooming schedule. Ear canals – particularly hairy and narrow ones – are generally warm and moist, making them a haven for bacteria. This can lead to repetitive ear infections and, in severe cases, the dog going deaf or requiring an operation to change the shape of his ear canal.

If your dog is a low or minimal shedder, the hair inside the ear flap should be regularly plucked. You can do this at home or ask your groomer to do it during routine visits. If you do pluck the hair yourself, don't overdo it, keep an eye out for redness or inflammation of the ear flap or inner ear. Ask your groomer for tips.

Some owners also regularly bathe the inner ear with cotton wool and warm water or a veterinary ear cleaner. If your Doodle's ears have an unpleasant smell, if he scratches them a lot or they look red, consult your vet as simple routine cleaning won't clear up an infection -and ear infections are notoriously difficult to rid the dog of once he's had one. Keeping your Labradoodle's ears clean and not too hairy is the best way to avoid infections starting in the first place.

Teeth cleaning

Veterinary studies show that by the age of three, 80% of dogs exhibit signs of gum disease. Symptoms include yellow and brown build up of tartar along the gum line, red inflamed gums and persistent bad breath. You can give your dog a daily dental treat such as Dentastix to help keep his mouth and teeth clean, but you should also brush your Doodle's teeth as well.

It shouldn't be a chore, but a pleasant experience for both of you. Take things slowly in the beginning, give him lots of praise and many dogs will start looking forward to teeth brushing sessions.

Use a pet toothpaste (the human variety can upset a canine's stomach); many have flavours which your Doodle will find tasty. The real benefit comes from the actual action of the brush on the teeth. Various brushes, sponges and pads are available, the choice depends on factors such as the health of your dog's gums, the size of his mouth and how good you are at teeth cleaning!

Get your dog used to the toothpaste by letting him lick some off your finger. If he doesn't like the flavour, try a different one. Continue this until he looks forward to licking the paste – it might be instant or take days. Put a small amount on your finger and gently rub it on one of the big canine teeth at the front of his mouth.

Then get him used to the toothbrush or dental sponge you will be using, praise him when he licks it – do this for several days. The next step is to actually start brushing! Talk to your Doodle in an encouraging way and praise him when you're finished.

Lift his upper lip gently and place the brush at a 45º angle to the gum line. Gently move the brush backwards and forwards. Start just with his front teeth and then gradually do few more. You don't need to brush the inside of his teeth as his tongue keeps them relatively free of plaque. Labradoodles love games and with a bit of encouragement and patience, it can become a fun task for both of you.

Nail Trimming

Nails must be kept short for the paws to remain healthy. Long nails interfere with the dog's gait, making walking awkward or painful. They can also break easily. This usually happens at the base of the nail, where blood vessels and nerves are located, and will require a trip to the vet's. If you can hear the nails clicking on the floor, they're too long.

To trim your dog's nails, use a specially designed clipper. Most have safety guards to prevent you from cutting the nails too short. You want to trim only the ends, before the "quick" which is a blood vessel inside the nail. (You can see where the quick ends on a white nail, but not on a dark nail.) Clip only the hook-like part of the nail that turns down. Many dogs dislike having their nails trimmed.

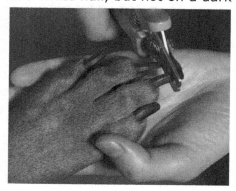

You can make it a painless procedure by getting him used to having his paws handled in puppyhood. Start trimming gently, a nail or two at a time, and your dog will learn that you're not going to hurt him. If you accidentally cut the quick, stop the bleeding with some styptic powder.

Another option is to file your dog's nails with a nail grinder tool. Some dogs may have tough nails which are hard to trim and this may be less stressful for your dog, with less chance of pain or bleeding.

If you find it impossible to clip your dog's nails, or you are at all worried about doing it, take him to a vet or a groomer.

Bathing

Your dog should have occasional, but not frequent, baths. Too frequent bathing removes natural oils and causes the coat to become dry and harsh. Use a mild shampoo specially formulated for dogs. Stand your dog in a tub, basin or bath and put cotton balls in his ears to keep them dry inside.

Wet him with warm water and apply shampoo from the neck back. Then put a small amount of shampoo on your hands and work it in to his head, making sure that you don't get any in his eyes. Rinse your dog thoroughly with warm water. Make sure you rinse down his nose; a dampened wash cloth over his eyes will help to keep the soap out. Rub dry with a towel (he'll help you with vigorous shaking!) and then blow-dry if necessary- and if he'll let you! Then give him a brush or a comb.

Eyes
If your dog has a discharge, if his eyes get a little sticky, or if he has dried deposits in the corner of his eyes, clean them gently with damp cotton wool. Do not use anything else unless instructed to do so by your vet.

Anal Glands
Anal glands are located on each side of your dog's anus (butt), they give off a scent when your dog has a bowel movement and squeezing them is normally done if you take your dog to a groomer's, as the glands can get full. If you notice your dog dragging himself along on his rear end or licking or scratching his anus, he may have impacted anal glands (or he may have worms or allergies).

Brushing and Combing
Scruffy Doodles will just need a good brush and comb once a week, whereas Doodles with fleece or wool coats will need an intensive grooming regime to avoid having to be clipped short.

Several brushing and combing sessions a week will keep the average Doodle neat and clean; daily attention is even better. Brush all the way down to the skin, letting the massaging action stimulate blood circulation and loosen and remove flakes of dandruff. Then go through the coat with a comb to make sure you have no mats or knots anywhere.

The kind of equipment you need depends on your Doodle's coat texture and length. Scruffy Doodles need pin brushes, which have long, round-ended stainless-steel or chrome-plated pins and a steel comb. Short and medium-coated Doodles will need bristle brushes and a comb.

For the fleece and wool coated Doodles you will need a slicker brush for removing mats and dead hair. Also a steel pinned comb to make sure that there are no tangles left. There are also rubber curry combs to polish smooth coats and remove dead hair; clippers, stripping knives, rakes, hair dryers, and other grooming tools.

When brushing, always check for burrs and other stubborn plant material, mats - which most frequently form behind the ears and under the legs - and any cuts or scrapes on the skin itself. Doodles shed, though some definitely shed more than others. Regular brushing will help keep shedding under control.

Grooming Kit

If you do decide to clip your Doodle yourself, this is a list of some of the things you may need:

- Pin Brushes or a Bristle Brush
- Slicker Brushes
- Rubber Curry Comb
- Metal Comb with fine and medium teeth
- Good Quality Scissors
- Dog Shampoo and Conditioner/Cream Rinse
- Ear Cleaner and Powder
- Cotton Wipes
- Nail Clippers
- Either Electric Clippers or a Stripping Knife
- A Grooming Table or Rubber Mat
- Possibly a Hair Dryer

If your Doodle visits the grooming salon every three or four months, then you should only need a brush, a comb, cotton wipes, shampoo and conditioner, a dog toothbrush and toothpaste.

The best grooming guide we have come across is from IDOG and we reproduce it here with their kind permission. You can copy it, fill it in and give it to your groomer.

Groomer Instructions
"The Doodle Do"
Full Coat Doodles

"Before"

Back, Torso, Chest and Neck
Trim to an even length on entire back, neck, chest and underbelly. No skirts.
(Select one)

❏   Cool Cut = 1 inch

Or

❏   Standard Cut = 2 inches

Torso Cut – Summer Cut

Legs
Trim to an even length on legs with a transition from torso to the legs. Transition should be smooth but not overly rounded.
(Select one)

❏   Cool Cut = 2 inches

Or

❏   Standard Cut = 3 inches

Feet
Hair should be brushed downward and then clipped to create a large round foot with a fluffy flared appearance. Do not clip short to the foot. Length of the hair can be a longer than the leg to create a flared and grounded effect. (Over sized slipper cut)
(Select none, one or both)

❏   Trim Foot Pad Hair (#10 or #15 Blade)

And/or

❏   Trim Nails

Foot Trim

Tail
Tail should have long wavy hair without a distinct appearance that it has been overly groomed. Base of tail should be trimmed and thinned to transition from body to tail.
(Select one)

❏   Trim Tail Hair To: _____ (length)

Or

❏   Do Not Trim Tail Length

Tail Trim

Private Parts
Area around the anus should not be overly trimmed to draw attention to it. Light haired doodles can have hair trimmed closer. Dark haired doodles should avoid short close trims to avoid light skin show through.
(Select one)

❏   Standard Short Sanitary Cut (#10 or #15 Blade)

Or

❏   Trim only around sexual organs. (No close cuts otherwise)

Head
Ears
Length of hair on the edges of the ears should only be trimmed slightly without a distinct appearance that they have been groomed. Trim should follow the curve of the ear.

(Select one)

❑ Trim Ear Hair Tips

Or

❑ Do Not Trim Ear Length

(Select one)

❑ Trim Inside Ear Hair

❑ Pluck Inside Ear Hair

❑ Do Not Trim or Remove Ear Hair

Optional

❑ Ear Channel: Trim hair under ear (where the ear lays) shorter. (For air flow around ear)

Eyes
Face should show eyes and have a smooth transition from face to top of head with a slight brow indication. (See Eye to Top of Head Transition Example)

(Select one)

❑ Trim between the eyes short. (Shown to the right)

Or

❑ Trim between the eyes but do not shave short to the skin (Dark Hair Dogs)

Optional

❑ Trim eyelashes

Nose and Beard
Nose and beard can be thinned to either a Cool trim or a Standard trim. It is best to also utilize thinning scissors to help with transitions from under neck and ear area. There should not be any abrupt cuts – transitions should appear smooth but not overly rounded. Do not use clippers.

(Select one)

❑ Cool Trim Nose and Beard – 2 inches – following the line of the mouth for the upper area nose trim ("C" cut). (Shown to the right – blonde dog)

❑ Standard Trim Nose and Beard – 3 inches

Optional

❑ Create an angular goatee type beard with an ending point. (Shown to the right)

Top of the Head
The puff on top of the head should look integrated with the body and neck of the dog. It should not appear to be overly rounded. Transition from eyes to top of head should show a slight brow (See Eye to Top of Head Transition Example) Avoid and overly groomed look. (Short, rounded top knot) Do not use clippers.

(Select one)

❑ Cool Top of the Head – 2 inches

❑ Standard Top of the Head – 3 inches

Eye to Top of Head Transition

Eyes Short Trim

Cool Trim Nose

Goatee

Top of Head

International Doodle Owners Group, www.idogrescue
Rescue, Education & Support © 2014

With thanks to the International Doodle Owners Group (IDOG) and The Doodle Trust (Labradoodle Trust) UK for assistance with this article.

12. The Birds and the Bees

Judging by the number of questions we receive from owners asking about breeding from dogs and the canine reproductive cycle, there is a lot of confusion about the doggie facts of life out there.

Some owners want to know whether they should breed from their dog, while others ask at what age they should have their dog spayed (females) or neutered (males).

If they have females they often ask when she will come on heat, how long this will last and how often it will occur. Sometimes they want to know how you can tell if a female is pregnant or how long a pregnancy lasts. So here, in a nutshell, is a short chapter on the facts of life as far as Labradoodles are concerned.

Breeding From Your Dog

Contrary to what you might think, breeding dogs is a complex issue – if you want healthy pups with good temperaments, that is. The pedigree breed societies discourage regular dog owners from breeding from their pets, as doing it properly is a business which requires specialist knowledge and testing.

The Labradoodle is a crossbreed and some people think that any Labrador and Poodle, or a male and a female Labradoodle, will all produce perfect Labradoodle pups. Sadly, this is not the case. The proper breeding of dogs is a demanding and expensive practice, requiring considerable knowledge. This should be backed up by genetic information and screening as well as a thorough knowledge of the desired traits of the breed - or crossbreed in the case of the Labradoodle.

The Australian Labradoodle Association is working towards getting an acceptable breed standard recognised for the Australian Labradoodle. This not only covers the physical size and appearance, but also temperament traits. One of the aims of any breed standard is to discourage indiscriminate breeding from owners who lack the necessary knowledge to breed excellent puppies. Casual breeding performed by friends or neighbours who happen to own Labradoodles, Poodles or Labradors seldom produces anything but mediocre Labradoodles.

It is not just about the look of the dogs; health, temperament and coat are important factors too. Many dog lovers do not realise that the single most important factor governing health and certain temperament traits is genetics.

Top breeders have years of experience in selecting the right pair for mating after they have considered the lineage, health, temperament, size and coats of the two dogs involved. If you are thinking of breeding from your dog, consider these questions:

* Are you 100% sure that your dog has no health or character problems which may be inherited by his or her puppies?

* Have you researched his or her ancestry to make sure there are no problems lurking in the background? Puppies inherit traits from their grandparents and great-grandparents as well as from the dam (female) and sire (male).

* Are you positive that the same can be said for the dog you are planning on breeding yours with?

* Have your dog, the mate and their parents all been screened for health issues which may be bred into Labradoodles, such as eye disease, hip and elbow dysplasia?

Our advice is that, unless you really know what you're doing and have some experience of breeding dogs, leave it to the experts.

Females and Heat

Just like all other animal and human females, a female Labradoodle also has a menstrual cycle - or to be more accurate, an oestrus cycle. This is the period when she is ready (and willing!) for mating and is more commonly called **heat** or being **on heat**, **in heat** or **in season**.

A female has her first cycle from about six months to one year of age. Small breeds like the Miniature Labradoodle tend to start early, but a large dog like a Standard Labradoodle may not begin her heat cycles until she is over one year old.

She will come on heat every six to eight months,

though the timescale becomes more erratic with old age and can also be irregular with young dogs when cycles first begin.

This will last on average from 12 to 21 days, although it can be anything from just a few days up to four weeks. Within that time there will be several days which will be the optimum time for her to get pregnant. This middle phase of the cycle is called the *oestrus.*

The third phase, called *diestrus*, then begins. During this time, her body will produce hormones whether or not she is pregnant. Her body thinks and acts like she is pregnant. All the hormones are present; only the puppies are missing. This can sometimes lead to what is known as a false pregnancy.

False Pregnancies

As many as 50% or more of intact (unspayed) female dogs may display signs of a false pregnancy. In the wild, it was common for female dogs to have false pregnancies and to lactate (produce milk). This female would then nourish puppies if their own mother died.

False pregnancies occur 60 to 80 days after the female was in heat - about the time she would have given birth – and are generally nothing to worry about for an owner. The exact cause is unknown. However, hormonal imbalances are thought to play an important role. Some female dogs have shown symptoms within three to four days of the surgical removal of the ovaries and uterus. Typical symptoms include:

- Mothering or adopting toys & other objects
- Making a nest
- Producing milk (lactating)
- Appetite fluctuations
- Barking or whining a lot
- Restlessness, depression or anxiety
- Swollen abdomen
- She might even appear to go into labour

Try not to touch your dog's nipples, as touch will stimulate further milk production. If she is licking herself repeatedly, she may need an Elizabethan collar (a large plastic collar from the vet) to minimize stimulation.

Under no circumstances should you restrict your female Labradoodle's water supply to try and prevent her from producing milk. This is dangerous, as she can become dehydrated.

Generally, females experiencing false pregnancies do not have serious long-term problems, as the behaviour disappears when the hormones return to their normal levels - usually in two to three weeks. However, some unspayed bitches may have a false pregnancy with each heat cycle.

Spaying during a false pregnancy may actually prolong the condition. Better to wait until the false pregnancy is over and then have her spayed to prevent it happening again. False pregnancy is not a disease, but an exaggerated response to normal hormonal changes. Owners should be reassured that even if left untreated, the condition almost always resolves itself.

However, if your Labradoodle appears physically ill or the behavioural changes are severe enough to worry you, visit your vet. He or she may prescribe tranquilisers to relieve anxiety or diuretics to reduce milk production and relieve fluid retention. In rare cases, hormone treatment may be necessary.

While a female dog is on heat, she produces hormones which attract male dogs. Because dogs have a sense of smell hundreds of times stronger

than ours, your female Labradoodle on heat is a magnet for all the males in the neighbourhood. They may congregate around your house or follow you around the park, waiting for their chance to prove their manhood – or mutthood in their case.

Don't expect your precious Labradoodle princess to be fussy. Her hormones are raging when she is on heat and during her most fertile days, she is usually ready, able and ...very willing!

As she approaches the optimum time for mating, your Labradoodle may bend her tail to one side. She will also start to urinate more frequently. This is her signal to all those virile male dogs out there that she is ready for mating.

The first visual sign you may notice is when she begins to lick her rear end – or vulva to be more precise. She will then bleed, this is sometimes called spotting. It will be a dark red at the beginning of the heat cycle, but the blood will become less and lighter in colour as the cycle evolves. With a small dog like a Miniature Labradoodle, there is not much blood. Obviously, there is more with a larger dog like the Standard Labradoodle.

Allowing your female to become pregnant during the first heat cycle is not recommended, as she is not yet mature and complications for the mother and puppies are more likely.

Unlike women, female dogs do not go through the menopause and can have puppies even when they are quite old. A first litter for an elderly female can also result in complications.

If you don't want your female Labradoodle to get pregnant, you should have her spayed.

In the United States and Europe, humane societies, animal shelters and rescue groups urge dog owners to have their pets spayed or neutered to prevent unwanted

Ad from an animal shelter

litters which contribute to too many animals in the rescue system or, even worse, having to be destroyed.

Normally all dogs from rescue centres and shelters will have been spayed or neutered. Many responsible breeders also encourage early spaying and neutering.

Spaying

Spaying is the term used to describe the removal of the ovaries and uterus (womb) of a female dog so that she cannot become pregnant. Although this is a routine operation, it is major abdominal surgery and she has to be anaesthetised.

A popular myth is that a female dog should have her first heat cycle before she is spayed, but this is not the case. Even puppies can be spayed. You should consult your vet for the optimum time, should you decide to have your dog done. One of the advantages is that, if done before the first heat cycle, your dog will have an almost zero risk of mammary cancer (the equivalent of breast cancer in women). Even after the first heat, spaying reduces the risk of this cancer by 92%.

Some vets claim that the risk of mammary cancer in unspayed female dogs can be as high as one in four. Some females may put weight on easier after spaying and will require slightly less food afterwards.

As with any major procedure, there are pros and cons. Spaying is a much more serious operation for a female than neutering is for a male. This is because it involves an internal abdominal operation, whereas the neutering procedure is carried out on the male's testicles, which are located outside his abdomen.

For:

- Spaying can reduce behaviour problems, such as roaming, aggression to other dogs, anxiety or fear.

- It prevents infections, cancer and other diseases of the uterus and ovaries.

- Your dog will have a greatly reduced risk of mammary cancer.

- Spaying reduces hormonal changes which can interfere with the treatment of diseases like diabetes or epilepsy.

- A spayed dog does not contribute to the pet overpopulation problem.

Against:

- Complications can occur, including an abnormal reaction to the anaesthetic, bleeding, stitches breaking and infections. This is not common.

- Occasionally there can be long-term effects connected to hormonal changes. These may include weight gain, urinary incontinence or less stamina and these problems can occur years after a female has been spayed.

- Older females may suffer some urinary incontinence. Some Standard Labradoodles may experience this, but it only affects a few spayed females. Discuss it with your vet.

If you talk to a vet or a volunteer at a rescue shelter, they will say that the advantages of spaying far outweigh any disadvantages. If you have a female puppy, you can discuss with your vet whether, and at what age, spaying would be a good idea for your Labradoodle when you take her in for injections.

Neutering

Neutering male dogs involves castration; the removal of the testicles. This can be a difficult decision for some owners, as it causes a drop in the pet's testosterone levels, which some humans – males in particular! - feel affects the quality of their dog's life.

Fortunately, dogs do not think like people and male dogs do not miss their testicles or the loss of sex! Our own experience is that our dog Max is much happier having been neutered. We decided to have him neutered after he went missing three times on walks – he ran off on the scent of a female on heat. Fortunately, he is micro-chipped and has our phone number on a tag on his collar and we were lucky that he was returned to us on all three occasions.

Unless you specifically want to breed from or show your dog, or he has a special job, neutering is recommended by animal rescue organisations and vets. Guide Dogs for the Blind, Hearing Dogs for Deaf People and Dogs for the Disabled are routinely neutered and this does not impair their ability to perform their duties.

There are countless unwanted puppies, especially in the USA, many of whom are destroyed. There is also the problem of a lack of knowledge from the owners of some breeding dogs, resulting in the production of puppies with congenital health or temperament problems.

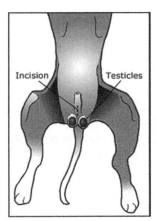

Neutering is usually performed around puberty, i.e. about six months old. It can, however, be done at any age over eight weeks, provided both testicles have descended. The operation is a relatively straightforward procedure.

Dogs neutered before puberty tend to grow a little larger than dogs done later. This is because testosterone is involved in the process which stops growing, so the bones grow for longer without testosterone.

The neutering operation for a male is less of a major operation than spaying for a female. Complications are less common and less severe than with spaying a female. Although he will feel tender afterwards, your dog should return to his normal self within a couple of days.

When he comes out of surgery, his scrotum (the sacs which held the testicles) will be swollen and it may look like nothing has been done. But it is normal for these to slowly shrink in the days following surgery. Here are the main pros and cons:

For:

- Behaviour problems such as roaming and aggression are usually reduced.

- Unwanted sexual behaviour, such as mounting people or objects, is usually reduced or eliminated.

- Testicular problems such as infections, cancer and torsion (painful rotation of the testicle) are eradicated.

- Prostate disease, common in older male dogs, is less likely to occur.

- A submissive entire (uncastrated) male dog may be targeted by other dogs. After he has been neutered, he will no longer produce testosterone and so will not be regarded as much of a threat by the other males, so he is less likely to be bullied.

- A neutered dog is not fathering unwanted puppies.

Cons:

- As with any surgery, there can be bleeding afterwards, you should keep an eye on him for any blood loss after the operation. Infections can also occur, generally caused by the dog licking the wound, so try and prevent him doing this. If he persists, use an E collar. In the **vast majority** of cases, these problems do not occur.

- Some dogs' coats may be affected, but supplementing their diet with fish oil can compensate for this.

Myths

Here are some common myths about neutering and spaying:

1. **Neutering or spaying will spoil the dog's character**
   There is no evidence that any of the positive characteristics of your dog will be altered. He or she will be just as loving, playful and loyal. Neutering may reduce aggression or roaming, especially in male dogs, because they are no longer competing to mate with a female.

2. **A female needs to have at least one litter**

There is no proven physical or mental benefit to a female having a litter. Pregnancy and whelping (giving birth to puppies) can be stressful and can have complications. In a false pregnancy, a female is simply responding to the hormones in her body.

3. **Mating is natural and necessary**
   Dogs are not humans, they do not think emotionally about sex or having and raising a family. Because Labradoodles like the company of humans so much, we tend to ascribe human emotions to them. Unlike humans, their desire to mate or breed is entirely physical, triggered by the chemicals called hormones within their body. Without these hormones – i.e. after neutering or spaying – the desire disappears or is greatly reduced.

4. **Male dogs will behave better if they can mate**
   This is simply not true; sex does not make a dog behave better. In fact it can have the opposite effect. Having mated once, a male may show an increased interest in females. He may also consider his status elevated, which may make him harder to control or call back.

Pregnancy

Regardless of whether you have a Miniature, Medium or Standard Labradoodle, a canine pregnancy will normally last for 61 to 65 days, typically 63 days. Sometimes pregnancy is referred to as the *gestation period.*

There is now a blood test available which measures levels of a hormone called *relaxin*. This is produced by the developing placenta and can be detected as early as 22 to 27 days after mating. The level of relaxin remains high throughout pregnancy and declines rapidly following whelping.

If your dog does not have a blood test, here are some of the signs of pregnancy:

- After mating, many females become more affectionate. (However, some will become uncharacteristically irritable and maybe even a little aggressive.) Watch out for any behavioural changes and contact your vet if you are concerned

- Your female may produce a slight clear discharge from her vagina about one month after mating
- Her appetite will increase in the second month of pregnancy
- She might seem slightly depressed and/or show a drop in appetite. This can also mean there are other problems, so you should consult your vet.
- Her teats (nipples) will become more prominent, pink and erect 25 to 30 days into the pregnancy. Later on, you may notice a fluid coming from them
- After about 35 days, or seven weeks, you will notice her body weight increase
- Her abdomen will become noticeably larger from around day 40, although first-time mums and females carrying few puppies may not show as much
- Many pregnant females' appetite will increase in the second half of pregnancy.
- Her nesting instincts will kick in as the delivery date approaches. She may seem restless or scratch her bed or the floor.
- During the last week of pregnancy, females often start to look for a safe place for whelping. Some seem to become confused, wanting to be with their owners and at the same time wanting to prepare their nest.

It is a good idea to get your pet used to the place where you want her to have her puppies well in advance of whelping. In spite of your good intentions, your Labradoodle may insist on having her puppies near you – and that might be on your bed in the middle of the night!

During Pregnancy

Females need special attention as well as a suitable diet during pregnancy. **Foods which are rich in calcium should not be fed during this time.** If you are feeding your pregnant Labradoodle a high quality premium dog food, a vitamin or mineral supplement may not be necessary. Some breeders add cottage cheese or a cooked egg to the diet every other day for extra protein.

Ever since I've started showing, my husband has affectionately called me "Three Humps"...

During the second half of pregnancy, you may also start adding small quantities of premium puppy food.

During the last week of pregnancy a female may eat two to four times the amount she ate before she was pregnant. As long as she is gaining a healthy amount of weight and not becoming obese, keep feeding her the increased amount. She should weigh the same at weaning as she weighed at breeding (providing this was her ideal weight).

Your female still needs daily exercise, but after the first month of pregnancy you should restrict vigorous activity and any agility events. You may consider supplementing her food at this stage. Do not give her too many supplements as this can be harmful to the developing puppies – check with your vet on what, if any, she needs as well as the correct diet.

In the sixth week, you should make or buy a whelping box and place it in a quiet area of your house – not the hall or the kitchen where people are in and out all the time. This is a box with a low side so she can get in and our easily with lots of old newspapers and old towels or a blanket in the bottom where your dog can give birth and which will be the puppies' first home. Whelping can be a messy business and the newspaper will help to absorb the fluids, which are normally green.

The whelping box should be big enough so that your female can stretch out, leaving plenty room for the puppies.

Some females stop eating during the last day of pregnancy, although this is certainly not the case with all. She will often go into a corner or a quiet room and start scratching or digging to make a bed. These signs may last for up to 24 hours and are part of the first stage of labour.

Some dogs like the owner to be with them the whole time they are in labour, while others prefer to have their puppies alone. If your pet chooses to be left alone, avoid intruding any more than absolutely necessary.

Females having puppies for the first time should be kept under surveillance until you think they have finished, just in case they get into trouble. Make sure your Labradoodle is properly caring for her newborn puppies, particularly if she is still in labour.

Some females are more concerned with straining to produce the next puppy than caring for the puppies already delivered. If that is the case, place the puppies in a small cardboard box containing a towel-wrapped bottle filled with warm (not hot) water, and covered with another towel to keep them warm and protected until the mother finishes delivery.

If your Labradoodle has produced at least one puppy and does not strain again within two hours, you should contact your vet as she requires medical assistance.

Ensuring that your pregnant female is properly looked after involves time and knowledge. We recommend that you consult your vet for advice and read as much as possible on the subject.

How Many Puppies?

Because there are so many variations with Labradoodles, the size of the litter can vary greatly. A general rule of thumb would be that a Labradoodle can have anything from four to a dozen puppies. Very young and elderly dogs usually have smaller litters.

13. Labradoodle Rescue

Are you thinking of adopting a Labradoodle from a rescue organisation? What could be kinder and more rewarding than giving a poor, abandoned Labradoodle a happy and loving home for the rest of his life?

Not much really, adoption saves lives. The problem of homeless dogs is truly depressing, particularly in the USA. The sheer numbers in kill shelters there is hard to comprehend. Randy Grim states in "Don't Dump The Dog" that 1,000 dogs are being put to sleep every hour in the States.

According to Jo-Anne Cousins, Executive Director at International Doodle Owners Group (IDOG), the situations leading to a Doodle ending up in rescue can be summed up in one phrase: unrealistic expectations.

She said: "In many situations, dog ownership was something that the family went into without fully understanding the time, money and commitment to exercise and training that it takes to raise a dog. While they may have spent hours on the internet pouring over cute puppy photos, they probably didn't read any puppy training books or look into actual costs of regular vet care, training and boarding.

"With doodles, many are going to homes that have never had a dog before because of allergies. The marketing of doodles as "hypo-allergenic" and/or non-shedding has caused a general misconception that *all doodles* are non-shedding, or will not cause allergies to flare up."

The most common reasons for rehoming are that the dog:

    * has too much energy and is knocking kids over and jumping on people

    * is growling and or nipping at the kids

    * chews or eats things it shouldn't

    * needs way more time and effort than the owner is able to or prepared to give

There is, however, a ray of sunshine for some of these dogs. Every year many thousands of people in North America, the UK and countries all around the world adopt a rescue dog and the story often has a happy ending.

The Dog's Point of View...

But if you are serious about adopting a Labradoodle, then you should do so with the right motives and with your eyes wide open. If you're expecting a perfect dog, you could be in for a shock. Rescue Labradoodles can and do become wonderful companions, but much of it depends on you.

Labradoodles are people-loving dogs. Many of them in rescue centres are traumatised. They don't understand why they have been abandoned by their beloved owners and in the beginning, may arrive with problems of their own until they adjust to being part of a loving family home again. Ask yourself a few questions before you take the plunge:

- Are you prepared to accept and deal with any problems - such as bad behaviour, shyness, aggression or making a mess in the house - which the dog may display when he initially arrives in your home?
- How much time are you willing to spend with your new pet to help him integrate back into normal family life?
- Can you take time off work to be at home and help the dog settle in at the beginning?
- Are you prepared to take on a new addition to your family that may live for another 10 years or so?

Think about the implications before taking on a rescue dog - try and look at it from the dog's point of view. What could be worse for the unlucky Labradoodle than to be abandoned again if things don't work out between you?

Other Considerations

Adopting a rescue dog is a big commitment for all involved. It is not a cheap way of getting a Labradoodle and shouldn't be viewed as such. It could cost you several hundred dollars - or pounds. You'll have adoption fees to pay and often vaccination and veterinary bills as well as worm and flea medication and spaying or neutering. Make sure you're aware of the full cost before committing.

Many rescue Labradoodles have had

difficult lives. You need plenty of time to help them rehabilitate. Some may have initial problems with housebreaking. Others may need socialisation with people as well as other dogs.

If you are serious about adopting, you may have to wait a while until a suitable dog comes up. One way of finding out if you, your family and home are suitable is to volunteer to become a foster home for one of the rescue centres. Fosters offer temporary homes until a forever home becomes available It's a shorter term arrangement, but still requires commitment and patience.

And it's is not just the dogs that are screened - you'll probably have to undergo a screening by the rescue organisation to ensure you are suitable. You might even have to provide references.

This is what the USA-based Doodle Rescue Collective Inc (DRC) has to say about fostering a Labradoodles, and most of the questions apply equally to anyone thinking of permanent adoption (with thanks to Jacquie Yorke):

"While it is noble, commendable and appreciated that you are considering becoming a temporary foster for DRC, we feel that it's important for you to understand the responsibilities involved with fostering a doodle. Once the initial emergency of saving a dog's life is past, fostering - like adoption - requires a tremendous amount of time, commitment, patience, flexibility and tolerance among other things. Fostering is not always easy.

"We hope that if you decide to foster for DRC that you will be willing to work with the dogs in your care and not only help them find their way to their new forever homes, but help them to also become wonderful family members.

"There are many reasons why a doodle ends up needing a new home. Some were purchased on a whim by people that didn't understand the temperament and needs of the breed. Sometimes lifestyle changes such as job loss or divorce are a factor in a dogs re-homing. Other doodles lose their homes when their owners become too sick or elderly to provide them with the necessary care. Sometimes owners are forced to enter an assisted-living facility or they pass away.

"Others are surrendered by people who just no longer want them. Regardless of the reasons why a doodle finds its way into rescue, the care that the dog will require while in a transitional foster home can at times involve more than just the provision of basic food, water and shelter.

"We are always looking for special loving foster homes and families that will provide not only the basics, but the extra care and attention that are sometimes necessary to insure that the doodles in our program become better companions and ultimately find their way to new forever homes.

Fostering Puppy Mill Survivors

"In the case of mill dogs, they have never had an actual home and are usually completely unfamiliar with human contact and life outside of their small cramped cages. Many have never felt the ground or grass beneath their feet. Many suffer from muscle atrophy and have never used their legs to do anything but stand within the confines of their cages. Many have never walked at all and need to learn how.

"Mill dogs are unfamiliar with human interaction, love, kindness, play, house manners etc. Many of these dogs were starved, physically abused, neglected and have had little or no veterinary care. They tend to be frightened, unsocialised, easily stressed and have difficulties with the concept of house training.

"Because of the lack of food available to them, many mill dogs have grown accustomed to eating their own feces and other non-edible substances. In most cases as a foster you will be providing these dogs with their very first experiences of life as a normal dog. Whatever the reasons, some doodles do come into rescue with "baggage." A foster home should be prepared for anything and have a basic understanding of the techniques used to help dogs in transition adjust.

What Will Be Expected of Me If I Decide to Foster for DRC?
"Fostering can involve house-training and/or crate training as well as introducing some basic obedience. Some will require special care, such as medical attention and you may be asked to take the foster dog to

scheduled veterinary appointments. It could require giving them medication at certain times of the day or perhaps bathing them periodically. They may need to increase their weight and/or strength.

Do you have a safe place to keep the rescue separate from the other animals in your home if necessary?
"The dog may need an area where it can be quarantined from other pets for approx. a week in case it has any types of infections etc that may be passed to your own animals. All of your own animals should be up to date on vaccinations (rabies, DHPP, bordatella), have monthly flea treatments,

209

and get along well with other animals.

Do you agree with crate training?
"You should be open to using a crate when you are not home or during the period of work on house-training as dogs often will find the crate a secure spot. You need to be familiar with how to properly use a crate.

Do you have a nice white carpet?
"Be aware that the many of the dogs will not be house-trained and will require work in that area. They may soil your carpets and other flooring so be prepared to clean up messes.

Do you have children? Are your children respectful around pets?
"Some dogs can easily be hurt by children who don't know how to treat them, while other dogs can be "over-enthusiastic" around small children, and are capable of knocking kids over while attempting to play. For the safety of both the dog and the children, we are quite cautious about placing dogs with families that have children under 12 years of age and generally will not place foster dogs in homes with very young children.

Are you willing to accept a dog with some behavioral issues?
"Some dogs have experienced emotional or physical trauma, while others have never received adequate socialization or training. Others have absolutely no issues. It depends on the dog and the circumstances.

Are you willing to surrender a dog to its new forever home even after you have created a strong bond with that dog?
"This is one of the most difficult aspects of being a foster caretaker, but it is inevitable. For many foster parents, the single biggest concern about fostering is falling in love. It takes a very special person to open their hearts to one of these dogs, to love and nurture them for a period of time, and then give them up when their new permanent home is found.

"We won't lie to you. There are usually some tears when your foster pet leaves, but there is also an immense feeling of satisfaction. It is especially rewarding to get an update from the new home and hear them brag about the most wonderful dog in the whole world, and know that it was your love and care that helped to make them such a special pet.

"Keep in mind, that if you choose to adopt a doodle that you're fostering, you may be at your limit of household pets and consequently you may not be able to continue to foster other doodles in need.

"When you foster a DRC doodle, you have the full support of the entire organization. We are always available to assist you and answer your questions and address your concerns at any time of the day or night. We in turn will rely on your experience and opinions when the time comes to select your foster doodle's new forever home.

"After all you know the dog, his or her issues, habits and personality best and we will always take your recommendations into consideration. DRC adopters and fosters alike become part of our BIG family so you will be able to stay in contact with your foster doodle's adoptive family and see that dog's progress.

"Please remember, it takes two weeks to a month for a dog to adjust to a new environment and it may not always be practical or possible to move a dog to another foster home at a moment's notice so you must be flexible. Still ready to foster? We hope so! We may not be able to save every doodle in the world, but we do mean the world to the ones we do manage to save."

If you haven't been put you off with all of the above..... Congratulations, you may be just the family or person that poor homeless Labradoodle is looking for!

 If you can't spare the time to adopt - and adoption means forever - you might want to consider fostering. Or you could help by becoming a fundraiser to generate cash to keep these very worthy rescue groups providing such a wonderful service.

However you decide to get involved, Good Luck!

Saving one dog will not change the world
But it will change the world for one dog

There are many dedicated people out there who give up their time free of charge to help find loving and permanent homes for dogs who would often otherwise be put down (euthanized). There are networks of these worthy people who have set up excellent rescue services for Labradoodles. Here are the main ones:

International Rescue Organisations

The International Doodle Owners Group, Inc (IDOG) Rescue was one of the first rescue groups to be set up. It is a highly-respected organisation with a network of Doodle owners committed to the protection of Labradoodles and Goldendoodles. They strive to keep Doodles out of shelters by helping to find new homes for them.

It is a not-for-profit 501(c) (3) public charity group based in the USA which has affiliations with Doodle owners' groups in other countries and is endorsed by both the Australian Labradoodle Association of America (ALAA) and the Goldendoodle Association of America (GANA).

It is an approved rescue partner in hundreds of shelters across the USA and has an excellent reputation for helping Doodles in need, having assisted more than 1,500 since starting. Adoption fees help to cover the costs of keeping the dogs and giving them the necessary medical treatment. These range from $100 to $750, depending on the individual dog - generally the younger the Labradoodle, the higher the fee.

IDOG Rescue has volunteers and foster homes across the USA, even internationally, operating without a shelter. As well as helping to rescue Doodles, IDOG states: "Our mission is to also provide education, resources and support to the owners and potential owners of Labradoodles and Goldendoodles to help them raise well-balanced, healthy dogs.

"IDOG offers counseling for behavioral issues and, when necessary, assists owners who want to rehome their dogs responsibly and safely."

Volunteers' aim is to get the dogs into homes that understand the temperament and needs of these energetic, playful and loving dogs. Any owner who finds they cannot keep their Labradooodle for whatever reason can contact the volunteers by emailing **rescue@idogrescue.com** for further advice.

IDOG is more than a rescue and education resource, the organisation fosters a spirit of cooperation and community among Doodle owners through social networking. It highlights social activities and get-togethers, as well as specialised interests such as agility, training, therapy dog volunteer activities and other service work.

It has this advice for prospective owners looking to provide a forever home:

"Seeing a dog in a photo is a great start to finding the right dog for your family, but please remember that our rescue coordinators have the very best understanding about what type of family and home environment will be most suitable for each individual dog.

"Very specific preferences will limit your chances: Sometimes people get distracted with what a dog looks like and often forget that there is a personality under all that fur. The perfect dog for you may be the opposite sex of the one you imagined. The right dog for your family might be black, or have a scruffy coat, or be a different age than you imagined.

"If you overlook some dogs because of sex, color or looks, you might just miss out on some great dogs. We urge you to consider all the dogs in our program based on their listing descriptions, and not on their photos. Please understand that our focus is on *rescuing* nice dogs and finding them good homes, not helping people find the picture-perfect dog that they can tell people they "rescued" because it is more socially acceptable.

"If your family really wants a puppy, or must have a blonde or female, or if your family has allergy issues to consider, our best recommendation is that you work with a responsible breeder to get exactly what you want. There is no shame in getting a pup from a responsible breeder.

"Please do not apply for a dog unless you are able and willing to travel to the foster's location to meet the dog. We rarely ship dogs and will do so only if we feel that it is the best option for the dog.

"Please realize that first-time dog owners comprise the majority of people who surrender dogs to shelters. For that reason, we are very hesitant to place a dog in a first time situation. Most rescue dogs need experienced owners."

IDOG Rescue does not place dogs in homes that use an electric fence or shock training collars, as they claim that this can spell disaster for rescue dogs.

If you meet the criteria and are still interested, visit the website at **www.idogrescue.com** where you will find a detailed application form to make sure you're a suitable candidate.

If fostering or adopting isn't an option for you, but you'd like to support their valuable work, you can donate online at: **www.idogrescue.com/index.php/support-idog/donate-to-idog-online**

North America

The Doodle Rescue Collective Inc. (DRC). Founded in 2008, it is a federally-recognised 501(c) (3) not-for-profit, charitable organisation. It does not have a shelter, but has built up a network of over 800 registered foster volunteers across the continent.

DRC is dedicated to the protection and rescue of Labradoodles and Goldendoodles in need and to the provision of educational resources and support services to Doodle owners, aspiring owners and enthusiasts. Through its programmes, it provides refuge, vet care, rehabilitation, transport and quality lifelong homes for Doodles in need. The driving force behind the organisation is joint founder member Jacqueline Yorke.

To date, DRC has saved over 1,000 Doodles through its successful and highly-regarded 'Rescue/Rehome Program.' The Collective has also assisted in the rescue, transport and responsible placement of hundreds of other Doodles in need since 2006. It is also endorsed by the Australian Labradoodle Association of America (ALAA), and the Goldendoodle Association of North America (GANA).

Doodle Rescue Collective Inc.can be found online at **http://doodlerescue.org** and is on Facebook and on Twitter @DoodleRescue If you would like to support this worthy cause, you can donate online at what has to be one of the longest URLs in cyberspace - **http://doodlerescue.org/opensocial/ningapps/show?appUrl=http%3A%2F%2Fos.ning.com%2Fningapps%2Fpaypal%2Fgadget.xml%3Fning-app-status%3Dnetwork&owner=1u68zgiy81vtj**
Or, if you are not reading this on a Kindle where you can just click through to the page, go to **http://doodlerescue.org** and click the **Donate** tab.

Oodles of Doodles Inc is also a Federal 501(c) (3) not-for-profit, charitable organization was set up in January 2009 and also operates in North America. It rescues Labradoodles, Goldendoodles, "fuzzy Terriers" and Schnoodles (crosses between Schnauzers and Poodles). As with IDOG and DRC, does not have a shelter, but uses its network of foster homes.

It states: "We are committed to our Foster Partners and in-home fostering. Our dogs are socialized, vetted and loved as part of the family.

Once adopted, our family and yours ensure our dogs continue to have the support of our Online Community. We will always be there for you and our dogs.

"We have also listed thousands of Oodles/Poodles/Doodles/Schnoodles seeking homes from all over North America. We can aid a family who needs to rehome their dog because of unforeseen circumstances or retiring breeder dogs."

"We are based in New Jersey but have dogs, fosters, rehomes and opportunities all over North America. Searchers wanted to help find listings for our site. Foster Partners wanted to help rescue more Oodles." In fact, all of the rescue organisations are looking for fosters to join their network.

Rather confusingly, the Oodles website is at **www.doodlerescuecollective.com** There is an ongoing dispute as to the ownership of the term 'Doodle Rescue Collective' – but whatever the ins and outs of it, the fact is that both organisations are striving to improve the outcomes for Labradoodles who have suffered the trauma of losing their families and homes through no fault of their own. You can shop and donate at the same time on the Oodles website at: **www.doodlerescuecollective.com/page/shop-to-donate**

UK

The main rescue organisation in the UK is the excellent Doodle Trust – a charity which changed its name from the Labradoodle Trust in 2014. It also rescues and rehomes Goldendoodles, Cockapoos, other Poodle crosses and Poodles.

The Trust is a first class resource for information for owners and prospective owners. It provides health and welfare advice as well as giving accurate information about the nature and behaviour of Poodle crossbreeds.

Volunteers are keen to educate owners BEFORE they get a Doodle to help prevent so many of these wonderful people-loving dogs being abandoned by their owners. Read **Chapter 1** of the Handbook to discover what questions the Trust believes you should ask before getting a Labradoodle – whether from a breeder or via a rescue organisation.

The Doodle Trust says: "We see educating the public about Doodles as a very important part of what we do. Unscrupulous breeders are continuing to mis-sell puppies as non-shedding and allergy friendly which is very misleading. This is also one of the main reasons these dogs are coming into rescue."

This is how the Trust works if an owner contacts them who is unable to keep the dog: "If it is decided that the best thing would be to sign the dog over to us, we will deal with this as quickly as we can. We do not charge to take dogs in and all of our dogs are fostered in a loving environment in people's own homes.

"Our kennels are only used in emergencies or for dogs that are unsafe to put into a family environment. The owner can keep in touch with the foster for progress reports if they so choose. However, we cannot divulge the name or address of the people who adopt from us.

"All dogs are fostered for a minimum of two weeks so that the foster can make a true assessment of the dog. If the dog has not been neutered already, we will have it done before it is rehomed. Once the dog has been assessed we look for a suitable home for it. The home must match the requirements of the dog. We do not rehome dogs to the first person that comes along.

"Once the potential new family has been found we contact them with details of the dog. If they are interested we then put them in touch with the foster so that they can learn more about the dog. During this time we will also arrange for somebody to home check the potential adopters. If the home check is passed and they like the dog they can then go ahead and meet it. If the meeting all goes well, they are given the opportunity to adopt the dog.

"Labradoodle Trust is committed to the welfare of any dogs that come into our care, and endeavours to make a positive contribution to their lives, no matter what the circumstances. We aim to educate people about Labradoodles BEFORE they take the plunge, and are often called by people wondering about their suitability to own one of these lively, intelligent dogs."

The Labradoodle Trust can be found online at **www.doodletrust.com** or, if not, at **www.labradoodletrust.com.** Click on their Just Giving page to find out how to donate to keep the good work of the Trust going – and you'll be rewarded with a free mention for your efforts.

This is by no means an exhaustive list, but it does cover some of the main organisations involved. Other online resources are the Pet Finder website at www.petfinder.com and Adopt a Pet site at www.adoptapet.com. There is also the Poo Mix site at http://poomixrescue.com. Many of the dogs listed with the Labradoodle-specific rescue organisations are also advertised on these websites.

If you do visit these websites, you cannot presume that the descriptions are 100% accurate. They are given in good faith, but ideas of what constitutes a medium dog and what is a small or large one may vary. Also

make sure you know what the different types of Labradoodle look like.

Some dogs advertised may be mistakenly described as "Poodle mix and Labrador" when they may have other breeds in their genetic make-up. It does not mean they are necessarily worse dogs, but if you are attracted to the Labradoodle for its temperament and other assets, make sure you are looking at a Labradoodle.

NEVER buy a dog from eBay, Craig's List, Gum tree or any of the other advertising websites which sell old cars, washing machines, golf clubs etc. You might think you are getting a cheap dog, but in the long run you will pay the price.

If the dog had been well bred and properly cared for, he or she would not be advertised on a website such as this. If you buy or get a free one, you may be storing up a whole load of trouble for yourselves in terms of behavioural, temperament and/or health issues due to poor breeding and/or training.

NB All the rescue dogs pictured in this chapter have been adopted.

14. Labradoodle Quiz

Questions

So, you think you know your Labradoodles? Well, here are 20 brainteasers to test the old grey matter. Answers are at the end.

1. What is a phantom Labradoodle puppy?

A)   A puppy which loves running round with a sheet over his head

B) A puppy which does not bark

C) A puppy which looks identical to either his deceased mother or father

D) A small, imaginary Labradoodle

E) A puppy with a solid base colour and a lighter face, chest and paws

2. According to Stanley Coren, PhD, Professor of Psychology at the University of British Columbia, what is the world's most popular name for a male dog in English-speaking countries? Is it:

A) Harley

B) Sammy

C) Buster

D) Max

E) Charlie

3. **Which of these breeds has webbed feet? Is it:**

   A) Newfoundland

   B) Standard Labradoodle

   C) Cocker Spaniel

   D) Duckhound

   E) Chihuahua

4. **According to the Australian Labradoodle Association, how tall should a fully-grown Standard Australian Labradoodle be at the withers (top of the shoulders)?**

   A) 15 to 18 inches

   B) 18 to 21 inches

   C) 21 to 24 inches

   D) 24 to 27 inches

   E) It varies, the colour is more important

5. **Humans have about 9,000 taste buds. How many do Labradoodles have?**

   A) 1,700

   B) 7,700

   C) 770,700

   D) 700,000

   E) 7 million

6. **What is the gestation period for Standard, Medium and Miniature Labradoodles? In other words, how long does a Labradoodle pregnancy last?**

A) One month

B) Two months

C) Three months

D) Four months

E) Five months

Ever since I've started showing, my husband has affectionately called me "Three Humps"...

7. What country did Labradoodles originate in?

A) USA

B) Canada

C) Great Britain

D) Australia

E) South Africa

8. Some Labradoodles may be hypoallergenic. What does this mean?

A) They are more likely to have allergies

B) They have low blood sugars

C) They are less likely to cause an allergic reaction in others

D) They are allergic to hypodermic needles and syringes

E) They are hyperactive

9. What type of dog does President Obama have?

A) A Standard Labradoodle

B) A Giant Schnoodle

C) A Giant Schnauzer

D) A Newfoundland

E) A Portuguese Water Dog

10. What is a parti Labradoodle? Is it:

A) One which has been crossed with a Parson Russell Terrier

B) A Standard Labradoodle crossed with a Mini Labradoodle

C) A coloured Labradoodle, normally with some white in his coat

D) One which shares a similar temperament to his mother

E) One which loves to go wild and drink cocktails with other Labradoodles, especially at night

11. Which of these famous people has a Labradoodle?

A) Cheryl Ladd

B) Barbara Streisand

C) Woody Allen

D) Beyoncé

E) Christina Aguilera

12. For what purpose were the first Labradoodles bred?

A) To hunt rabbits and other small animals

B) As therapy dogs in hospitals

C) As retrieving dogs on game shoots

D) As guide dogs for the blind

E) As mountain and water rescue dogs

13. Some Labradoodles may suffer from a genetic disease called PRA. What does this stand for?

A)   Persistent Renal Agitation

B)   Progressive Retinal Atrophy

C)   Pernicious Regressive Anemia

D)   Pseudo Rabies Ataxia

E)   Persistent Repeated Angina

14. The first Labradoodle was bred in the 1980s by a person called:

A) Jasper Conran

B) Wally Conron

C) Wally Hammond

D) Wares Wally

E) Babs Doodle

15. The first recorded Labradoodle was bred from a Standard Poodle called Harley and a Labrador called Brandy. What was the Labradoodle's name?

A) Susan

B) Suleman

C) Sultan

D) Summer

E) Sonny

16. The Labradoodle is a mix of Labrador and Poodle. In which country did the Poodle originate?

A) Germany

B) Great Britain

C) Australia

D) Belgium

E) France

17. What is a parchment Labradoodle?

A) One which has a leathery skin like a calf

B) A bald one

C) A Labradoodle which can read and write

D) A Labradoodle with a dry skin problem

E) A coffee-coloured Labradoodle

18. On which island did the modern Labrador originate?

A) Ireland

B) Greenland

C) Iceland

D) Newfoundland

E) Scotland

19. If not properly trained and allowed to get away with things, some small dogs like Miniature Labradoodles can develop "Little Emperor" tendencies. Does this mean?

A) They like dressing up in fancy clothes

B) They start ordering other Labradoodles around

C) They try to take over other Labradoodles' beds and toys

D) They will only eat very expensive food

E) They become cocksure and behave badly

20. Which of these foods is poisonous to dogs?

A) Grapes

B) Chocolate

C) Onions

D) Macadamia nuts

E) Alcohol

Answers

1. E – it's a colour. The phantom Labradoodle has a solid base colour with sharply defined markings of a second colour appearing above each eye, on the sides of the muzzle, on the throat and fore chest, or in a chin and fore chest bowtie pattern as well as on all four legs and feet and below the tail.

2. D – Max. The second most popular is Jake. The most popular name for a female is Molly, followed by Bella. The names Rover, Fido, Bowser and Lassie do not make the top 50.

3. A – Newfoundland. Many of the dogs with webbed feet were bred by hunters to swim and retrieve ducks and other waterfowl.

Other dogs with webbed feet include the Akita, Brussels Griffon, Chesapeake Bay Retriever, Chinook, Field Spaniel, German Short Haired Pointer, German Wire Haired Pointer, Irish Water Spaniel, Labrador Retriever, Leonberger, Newfoundland, Nova Scotia Duck Tolling Retriever, Otterhound, Plott Hound, Portuguese Water Dog, Redbone Coonhound, Spanish Water Dog, Weimaraner and Wire Haired Pointing Griffon. There is no such dog as a Duckhound.

4. C - 21 to 24inches, (not over 25") or 53cm to 63cm. The ideal size for the female is 21 to 23 inches and the male is 22 to 24 inches. The weight should be 23kg to 30kg (50-65lbs), although some are larger.

5. A - 1,700, which is the same as all other dogs. Cats only have about 470. However, if you often wondered why your Labradoodle enjoys drinking from muddy puddles instead of his metal bowl, it is because he enjoys the flavour. He has taste buds for water, something we do not have.

6. B - Two months or 61 to 65 days, regardless of whether the Labradoodle is a Miniature, Medium or Standard.

7. D – Australia. The Labradoodle became known in 1988 when breeder Wally Conran crossed the Labrador and Standard Poodle at the Royal Guide Dogs Association of Australia in Victoria.

His aim was to combine the low-shedding coat of the Poodle with the gentleness and trainability of the Labrador to provide a guide dog suitable for people with allergies.

8. C - They are less likely to cause an allergic reaction in others.
Hypoallergenic dogs are generally low or virtually non-shedding and they do not usually cause people with allergies to have a reaction. (No dog is

guaranteed 100% not to cause a reaction, as allergies vary from person to person).

9. E – A Portuguese Water Dog called Bo. He is a neutered male born in October 2008. The Obama family were given Bo as a gift after months of speculation about a hypoallergenic dog. The final choice was made partly because Malia Obama has allergies.

10. C - A coloured Labradoodle. These days partis come in a range of different colours, but one of the colours is always white. "Parti" comes from the French word for *divided* and means two colours. Parti Labradoodles are at least 50% white.

11. A - Cheryl Ladd. The former Charlie's Angel has a Standard Labradoodle called Crockett who loves to sing. Cheryl said: "He looks like a giant polar bear. He's kind of a bombshell blonde and just full of love. He's got big amber eyes and a great big liquorice nose and we're just madly in love with him."

12. D – As guide dogs for the blind. See answer 7.

13. B - Progressive Retinal Atrophy. This is a hereditary disease of the eye carried by a recessive gene in some Poodles and Labradors.

There are various ways of testing a dog for hereditary eye conditions; the OptiGen prcd-PRA Test and Canine Eye Registration Foundation (CERF) in the USA and the British Veterinary Association (BVA) Eye Test in the UK.

14. B - Wally Conron. After receiving a request from a blind woman living in Hawaii who needed a guide dog that wouldn't aggravate her husband's allergies.
Wally crossed a Labrador with a Standard Poodle to produce a litter of three Labradoodle puppies, only one of which didn't bother the husband's allergies. The other two puppies also lived useful lives.

15. C - Sultan. He had a good temperament and was very friendly. Wally Conron trained Sultan for 18 months before shipping him to his new home in Hawaii.

16. A - Germany. The Poodle is actually a German breed. Its name comes from the Old German word 'pudeln' meaning to splash in puddles. The breed was standardised in France, where it was commonly used as a water retriever. Due to the breed's popularity, it became established as France's national breed.

17. E. A rare parchment Labradoodle is a creamy beige chocolate colour, like café au lait. Puppies are born with a coat the colour of milk chocolate that lightens over time.

18. D - Newfoundland, now part of the province of Newfoundland and Labrador, Canada. The founding breed of the Labrador was the St John's Water dog, a breed created by the island's 16th century settlers.

This dog's ancestors were likely a random mix of English, Irish and Portuguese working breeds. The Newfoundland breed is probably a result of the St. John's Dog breeding with mastiffs introduced by Portuguese fishermen.

19. E - They become cocksure and behave badly. As a result of being pampered or spoilt, they think that they rule the roost and begin to behave badly. When this happens, a firm hand is needed along with some training sessions.

20. All of them.

The End – how many did you get right?

A Happy Ending

The following amusing account is from Amy Vansant, who lives in Maryland with her long-suffering husband, Mike, and their beloved Labradoodle, Gordon:

Man's Best Friend?

This quote is the source of some arguing. My husband, Mike, and I work from home, which gives us a lot of quality time together.

A *lot* of quality time. A *whole lot* of quality…

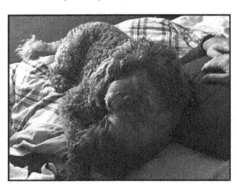 OK, *fine*. We argue. Actually, we bicker. We bicker over trivial things because we can't get out of each other's way. For instance, he'd like to know why I have four glasses of water on my bedside table, filled to various depths. Do I think I'm going to wake up in the middle of the night desperate to play a few Christmas carols on a glass xylophone?

I want to know why he can't finish everything on his plate. Why does he *always* leave 1/4 of a sandwich? Does he think he has to leave a little food on the plate so it can spawn the *next* meal? He knows that isn't how food works, right?

But the thing we bicker the most about is our dog, Gordon the Labradoodle. Who loves him more?

Dog is man's best friend? Not on my watch.
If Gordon coughs or licks or makes any sort of strange breathing noise in the middle of the night, we start a battle as to why.

"He's going to throw up," says Mike.

"No, that's just his throat clearing noise," I say. "He's fine."
Granted, this may be more wishful thinking than science.

"Is there a towel nearby?" mumbles Mike, pretending he's too asleep to find one himself. Daniel Day-Lewis should be glad Mike wasn't nominated for the Oscar this year.

"Probably, but he's fine."

I try and go back to sleep, only to hear Gordon's tell-tale *hoomph* *hoomph* *hoomph* barf noise begin at the foot of the bed.

"He's throwing up! YES! I TOLD YOU!" Mike announces triumphantly as I lunge for a towel to catch the vomit before it hits the comforter.

"Mommy would never get that excited about you throwing up," I whisper to the dog as I wipe off his mouth, proving to him I love him more.

If dog is man's best friend, maybe his best friend could catch the vomit once in a while.

In the morning, tired and cranky, we bicker about why the dog is staring at us.

"He has to go out," says Mike.

"He was just out," I say. "He's bored. He wants to play."

"I don't think he pooped," says Mike. "He has to go out."

If Mike and I were on *Family Feud* and the topic was "Things Amy and Mike Talk About" ....Survey SAYS!

Things Amy and Mike Talk About

"What do you want for dinner?"
"I don't know. What do you want for dinner?"

"I think the dog has to poop."

"What do you want to watch?"
"I don't care. What do you want to watch?"

Kid-FreeLiving.com

As Mike grills me to remember the last time the dog went to the bathroom, Gordon trots off and returns with his favorite ball in his mouth.

"YES! In your *face*!" I'll say, doing my most obnoxious victory dance. "He wants to *play*. I know my dog better than you."

"Right," Mike says, brushing off his defeat. "Not even *close*."

When it comes to our furry baby, the one thing Mike and I agree upon is that we don't know what we'll do without him. Gordon's eyes are starting to get that old-dog cloudiness. He's eight now, and we're starting to get more nervous every year.

"I don't know what I'll do when he dies," says Mike as we share some wine on the sofa. "I'll probably just die, too."

"Me too," I say, petting the furry old man on my lap. Gordon. Not Mike.

"You'll be fine. I love him more than you," says Mike. "It's over for me when he goes."

I snort in disagreement. "You do *not* love him more than me."

"Yes I do."

"No you don't."

We look at Gordon with tearing eyes. We sigh. We stop bickering. The dog gets uncomfortable with the melodramatic, wine-induced love-fest, gets up and stand by the door. He lets loose a huffy little bark.

"He has to poop," says Mike, wiping his eyes with a strong, manly gesture.

"No, he wants to get the paper," I say, because I know Gordon, and he loves me more.

Charles the Lion King

The first caller was fairly calm. "I'd like to report a lion sighting," he said.

"Say that again?" a dispatcher responded. And thus began the drama over baby lion sightings in Norfolk, Virginian.

The first call came at 10:19 a.m. The animal was running on Granby Street, a male voice said. Then a woman took the phone. She sounded anxious as she described the proximity to the zoo.

"There was a lion that ran across the street. A baby lion. It was about the size of a Labrador retriever. It's roaming loose in the neighborhood."

A second call came five minutes later. "I just saw an animal that looked like a small lion. It had the mange and everything," a man said. "I don't know if it got away from the zoo, or what," he said.

A third call came at 1:19 p.m. "I just saw a baby lion at Colley Avenue and 50th Street," a man reported. "What kind of animal?" the dispatcher later asked him.

"A lion. A baby lion, maybe." The lion was going to nearby houses. "I don't think it has caused any problem so far," said the caller.

"OK. You think it's looking for food?" the dispatcher asked. "I don't know."

These were the frantic 911 calls reporting rare and frightening sightings to Norfolk Emergency Operation Center. One caller after another reported sighting a small lion on the prowl.

The centre went on alert, staff needed to ensure that there was no wild animal on the streets. Norfolk police put in a call to the local zoo to make sure one of its lions hadn't made a daring escape.

The zoo said that all their lions were accounted for; all present and correct...and, as it turns out, it wasn't the King of the Jungle on the loose after all.

The "baby lion" was none other than an exotically-coiffured three-year-old Labradoodle called Charles the Monarch with a rather luxurious "mane."

His owners Daniel and Natalie Painter had actually had him trimmed specifically to look like a lion -although they had no idea of the consequences when they did it.

Their daughter was going to school at Old Dominion University - their football team mascot is a lion and their nickname is The Monarchs. Without telling anybody, they took Charles to the dog groomer's and asked for him to be trimmed like a lion.

Charles has taken it all in his stride. The Painters describe him as: "Casual, laidback. He does whatever he needs to. He's just your everyday party animal." Although Daniel added: "I tell people he's a Lab-a-lion, and half the people really believe that!"

Since being mistaken for a lion, Charles has made headlines around the world and become an internet sensation. The King of the Canines has gone viral - the morning after the incident was reported, Charles had more than 11,000 likes on his Facebook page. He has appeared on "Good Morning America," has become popular as far away as Germany and Japan, and is now the subject of a children's book.

Charles frequently attends football tailgates, posing with fans and the actual Old Dominion mascot Big Blue. There has been a petition to make Charles an official mascot of the school, but for now it's just a pet project...In fact, he doesn't look like a ferocious lion at all... does he?!?

Shadow's Story

In February 2012, IDOG Rescue received a call from a woman in Texas, desperate to find a safe haven for her two-year-old Labradoodle.

The woman was a victim of domestic abuse who had fled from the home with her young son, but was not able to take Shadow with her. Her husband had threatened that Shadow needed to be gone that day "or else…"

A very kind hearted woman heard of Shadow's plight and offered his owner help by collecting Shadow and keeping him safe until he could be taken into foster care. She was a person used to dealing with difficult situations and a very capable dog handler. She took Shadow home for a couple of nights, and then met an IDOG Rescue volunteer to hand him over.

"This is the saddest dog I have ever seen," she said. Poor Shadow was absolutely distraught. There was not a glimmer of hope in his eyes, and his tail and head hung low. He had to be carried from one vehicle the other.

Once safely in the foster home, Shadow was quickly accepted by the foster's own two Labradoodles. They seemed to sense that Shadow needed encouragement. Shadow was hesitant and fearful, just quietly watching the foster's dogs interact with the foster.

Slowly, his tension eased enough for him to eat a little and sleep. He was sweet, but never truly relaxed. Sudden noises startled him and people entering the house would send him into a frightening barking frenzy, even if he knew who the people were. He was especially wary of men.

Shadow was a black flat-coated Labradoodle with interesting silver colouring on his eyebrows and muzzle that made him look older than his young age. He shed lightly, and did not have ideal body shape. In short, not what most adopters were looking for. The behavioural issues on top of that gave us little hope that he would be adopted easily or quickly.

He was an extremely sweet dog, with brown eyes that could melt your heart. He was safe with IDOG for as long as he needed.

Almost three months passed when suddenly, out of the blue, came a ray of hope. A woman in Michigan had seen Shadow's listing and felt a connection with this sweet boy. She was prepared to fly down to Texas, rent a car and drive him back to Michigan, using the trip as bonding time.

We began the adoption application process trying to keep our excitement and hope under control. The application seemed too good to be true – Shadow would have a lovely family who would accept him and love him for his sweet self, warts and all!

Shadow's family do whatever they can to make his life free from anxiety. They are encouraging and patient. His Doodle brother Roscoe adores him. They play for hours and Shadow continues to grow more confident and sure of his place in the world.

He is loved ... he is safe.

THE END

Useful Contacts

The Labradoodle Trust (lots of useful info for prospective and current owners)
www.labradoodletrust.com Due to change name later in 2014 to **The Doodle Trust** www.doodletrust.com

Australian Labradoodle Association of America http://alaa-labradoodles.com

Australian Labradoodle Club of America
www.australianlabradoodleclub.us

The UK Labradoodle Association www.labradoodle.org.uk

Australian Labradoodle Association (Australia) www.laa.org.au

Labradoodles (forum, set up by breeders) http://labradoodle-dogs.net

Goldendoodles (info and forum on all types of Doodle, set up by breeders) http://goldendoodles.com

IDOG (International Doodle Owners Group) Lots of useful info and rescue www.idogrescue.com

Doodle Rescue Collective Inc http://doodlerescue.org

Oodles of Doodles Rescue Collective www.doodlerescuecollective.com

The Doodle Zoo (owners' very sociable forum) www.thedoodlezoo.com

Doodle Kisses (social networking site for Labradoodle and Goldendoodle owners) www.doodlekisses.com

DoodleSport (Labradoodle gifts) www.doodlesport.com

Doodle Country (Grooming tools, toys, etc) http://doodlecountry.com

Kid Free Living (amusing blog on living with a Labradoodle)
www.kidfreeliving.com

Pet insurance USA www.consumersadvocate.org/pet-insurance/best-pet-insurance.html

Pet insurance UK www.which.co.uk/money/insurance/reviews-ns/pet-insurance

There are also several groups on Facebook, many organise Doodle romps.

Disclaimer

This book has been written to provide helpful information on Labradoodles. It is not meant to be used, nor should it be used, to diagnose or treat any medical condition. For diagnosis or treatment of any animal medical problem, consult a qualified veterinarian. The author is not responsible for any specific health or allergy conditions that may require medical supervision and is not liable for any damages or negative consequences from any treatment, action, application or preparation, to any person reading or following the information in this book. References are provided for informational purposes only and do not constitute endorsement of any websites or other sources.